Memoir of a Park Avenue
BASSET HOUND

Memoir of a Park Avenue
BASSET HOUND

How a South Jersey Hound Found True Love on the Upper East Side

by Amelia Rowley

as told to Peter Rowley

Archway Publishing books may be ordered through booksellers or by contacting:

Archway Publishing
1663 Liberty Drive
Bloomington, IN 47403
www.archwaypublishing.com
1-(888)-242-5904

ISBN: 978-1-4808-1324-3 (sc)
ISBN: 978-1-4808-1775-3 (hc)
ISBN: 978-1-4808-1323-6 (e)

Library of Congress Control Number: 2014920905

Print information available on the last page.

Archway Publishing rev. date: 6/1/2015

To the memory of Flora

ACKNOWLEDGMENTS

I would like to thank the following humans and one cockerpoo for helping me write my memoir: Peter Rowley read my thoughts and told my story. He also took most of the pictures because my paws were too big to press the right buttons and levers on the camera. I am especially grateful to Terez Rowley for her love and support throughout the project. Without her hugs and kisses, this book could never have been written. I am grateful to Caroline Rowley; Letitia; Sheila; and my special friend, Bo. May his tail wag forever!

CONTENTS

A Dramatic Birth 1
Park Avenue 4
Flora Rowley 10
You Ain't Nothing But a Hound Dog 15
A Giant Dog Next Door 17
The Toy Store 20
Puff Daddy 25
Letitia 29
Getting Older 31
Daily Life 37
True Love 62
Escape from Death 77
No More Bo 103
Further Adventures 121
Epilogue: Peter's Story 132

Me and Caroline's Legs

A DRAMATIC BIRTH

I was born on a ticky-tacky basset hound farm in South Jersey, surrounded by elm trees, long grass, muddy fields, and unkempt bushes, but I have since risen in the world. When I was born, my two brothers, two sisters, and mother died.

It was a cold and snowy night. The wind was whistling through the big elms on the O'Dell farmstead. As I peeked around one of my soft floppy ears, I could see four other baby bassets and my mother lying on straw.

A female human voice above me, belonging to its fat frowzy owner, said in a harsh South Jersey twang, "They're dead. Goddammit. Except for one!"

A male voice uttered a string of words, which were so profane that to this day, I blush at the very memory of them.

"The sooner we sell her, the better," said the woman.

The lights went out, and I was left alone to cry over my siblings and mother as the curses grew fainter in the darkness. Their bodics were very still.

The next day, an unfamiliar man appeared with a large plastic bag and a shovel and took their bodies. I was left alone in my cage except for the sound of the birds in the trees and dogs yapping in other cages. The iron door of my cagc then opened, and a bottle with a rubber tip was shoved in my mouth.

"She's a pretty little thing," said Mrs. O'Dell to no one in particular. "We should be able to get a thousand dollars for her. She's pedigree." I had no idea what she meant. I could hear the dogs in other cages and wished my brothers, sisters, and mommy were alive.

Four months later, I heard a car drive up. I had grown considerably. I waddled on my short stumpy legs to the edge of my cage.

"I'll sell her to you at a discount price—only a thousand dollars. She's got all her shots, and she'll be trained in a month," I heard Mrs. O'Dell say. I knew the last basset hound puppy had been sold for seven hundred dollars. I had no idea what she meant by being *trained.*

Looking into my cage were two strangers and Mrs. O'Dell, her arms crossed over her substantial chest.

One of the strangers was a blonde, middle-aged lady (she wore only a small amount of lipstick compared to Mrs. O'Dell's, who looked as if her makeup had been laid on with a spade and whose hair had been lacquered into an immovable bush), and the other was a very pretty teenage girl in blue jeans and a blouse that fitted her young body well.

"She's adorable," said the lady who sounded different from the other humans I had heard.

"She looks just like Flora as a puppy," said the girl in an American voice.

I heard later that the husband of the blonde lady with the mellifluous voice (she turned out to be of Hungarian origin, by the way) had stayed in their car, depressed by the very thought of my becoming a member of his upmarket family.

The next thing I knew, I was flopped down (I weighed only fifteen pounds then) on the style section of the *New York Times* in the back of an SUV. My new owners had placed me there. "If we shut the rear door, she won't escape," I heard one of them say.

It was a very warm sticky afternoon, and we were heading north on the Jersey Turnpike to New York City, where I currently reside. When we stopped at a gas station near Exit 9, I could smell burgers and hot dogs from the nearby fast-food restaurants. I did not like the idea of dogs being burned on a hot summer day. It was only later I learned that hot dogs were not made out of baby bassets and other breeds. What a relief that was because I had not been well-treated at the O'Dell kennels, and I was afraid of many things.

PARK AVENUE

The Lincoln Tunnel into New York was very dark, noisy, and frightening. Lights kept flashing by. But my new family—a father, a mother, and their teenage daughter—did not seem to be bothered. They said their name was Rowley, and the daughter, Caroline, called me Amelia. I like the sound of that, with the A's at the beginning and end sounding like a stream bubbling down a hill. Since there was nowhere else to go, I peed on the style section of the newspaper. I heard Mrs. Rowley say, "Ugh."

Caroline exclaimed, "There's a smell!" What did they expect? Chanel No. 5?

I was surprised by the bright lights of Broadway when we came out of the tunnel, and the noise from the cars and people was like nothing I had ever heard outside of Gibbsboro, New Jersey. I was glad to see dogs on the sidewalk, although I didn't see why they had to have leashes around their necks.

In South Jersey, I had lived in a cage. Mr. O'Dell would prod me with a pitchfork when cleaning out my pen, forcing me to move. I would snarl, but he paid no attention, as he had boots on. I was too short to bite as high as his knees, which were always covered by a pair of mud-splattered black denims.

After we crossed town on Forty-Second Street, we drove up Park Avenue, which was a vast improvement over Gibbsboro, although the tall apartment buildings seemed very forbidding. I saw a full-grown basset hound in a group of dogs being marched along by a woman. The basset, the German shepherd dog, the Pomeranian, and the poodles acted very superior, and their fur was clean and lovely. Would I fit in? Could I escape? Did I want to?

Why was I so beautiful? Could it be the result of my moderate lifestyle and diet of only two meals a day? Was it genetics? Why were my ears and body so long, my legs so short, and my brain so small? One of my favorite habits was drinking my pee. The O'Dells never stopped me.

"That's one way to clean it up," I had heard Mrs. O'Dell say.

Upon my arrival at 815 Park Avenue, I quickly discovered that Caroline and Mr. Rowley do not like me to do this when they take me outside. Mrs. Rowley said within earshot, "The vet told me that bassets are the only breed with this characteristic." However, I heard Mr. Rowley say that the Indian prime minister drank his No. 1 when he visited Jimmy Carter in the White House.

It took me a while to adjust to Park Avenue. Except for the few trees, brown grass, and flowers in the center median, there was concrete and glass as far as my eye could see. The only concrete on the farm outside of Gibbsboro had been the small patch between my cage and the others.

There were doormen in front of every apartment building entrance. There had not been a single doorman by the gate to the dirt track that led to my basset farm. The doormen were very polite to me, unlike the owner and his wife at my first home, who frequently used words about me and the dogs in the other cages that could not possibly appear in a family newspaper.

I am told silken words are *de rigueur* on Park and Fifth Avenues. Where did I learn French? That's my secret. Bassets are very bright. In our building, I heard Ramazan, a tall man from Montenegro who wore a dark blue uniform with cap, say ironically of a wolfhound walking past our entrance, “A typical Park Avenue dog. They’re treated better than we are.”

He smiled when he saw me amble by. I like Ramazan already.

I am lonely. I meet other Amelias in the elevator.

However, one thing reminded me of South Jersey: I had to go up and down to the Rowleys’ fifteenth floor apartment by the service elevator. I felt dogs were treated with the same lack of respect at

815 Park that the O'Dells had shown their four-legged wards on the farm. With Mr. Rowley's help, I soon learned to keep my handsome tail out of the elevator door. He would pull me by the neck so that I was forced to move a foot forward. A few months earlier, a small dog had lost its tail when the door closed!

There was a nice view from their apartment, but I could see only the sky because I was so short. The elevator floor and walls were bare and smelled of other dogs, which I enjoyed. I was a keen sniffer and spent many minutes scouring the mottled linoleum floor for food and the odors of my fellow canines. I was told dogs were not allowed in the passenger elevators.

When I arrived, I was introduced to a black cat with white chin and socks, Pokey, who apparently lived there. I growled in my most fearsome way at this feline. Pokey retreated, hissing.

I heard that as a result of my behavior, Pokey was given to a nice family in Bayside, Queens. Caroline said, "It was either the cat or the dog. Amelia cost us a lot of money, whereas we got Pokey for nothing as a kitten seven years ago. Anyway, there is more of Amelia than Pokey. And dogs are friendlier than cats." I quite agree. How my predecessor, Flora, survived with the two cats, Pokey and Tilly, I do not understand. Maybe it was because she was English and did not have such high standards.

Mrs. Rowley, who served on the board of my building, said, "Only one dog is allowed per apartment." I wished 815 Park did not have such a rule, because it makes life rather lonely. I would like to have had another basset—preferably a male—as a companion. Mrs. Rowley added, "However, we allow two cats in each apartment." Why was I being discriminated against? Should I have gone to an animal rights lawyer?

One of the first things the Rowleys did was to fix me, but I still like sex. Fixing was not a pleasant experience, though I was given a painkiller by the vet and knocked out after an injection. I developed a hatred for the vet's office down on Seventy-Sixth Street. Anyway, at least I don't have to worry about an unwanted pregnancy, and considering what happened to my mother and siblings, maybe it is all for the best.

I suppose it was partly my fault that there were no other animals in our apartment, except for the cockroaches. As they were afraid of me, they stayed out of sight. I heard Mr. Rowley say, "When there's a cat or a dog in the apartment, the cockroaches stay hidden in the walls." Mr. Rowley, I knew, didn't like to let the exterminator in our apartment, as he was afraid of being poisoned by the very poison used on the cockroaches. Mrs. Rowley disagreed with him on this.

Occasionally, I was allowed to travel in the main elevator when the service elevator was down for maintenance and repairs, which was actually quite often. The humans' elevator had a shiny brass handrail, which was of no use to me. Within twelve months, I had grown to be one and a half feet tall, and my body from my brown and white tail to my black wet nose was four feet long. Even though I was long and low, I would have been glad to challenge any other dog or human to a foot race.

Mr. Rowley says, "Bassets were the poor man's hunting dogs. They ran along low to the ground. Their ears, trailing on the earth and grass, were able to pick up the sounds of rabbits." I did not like to think of myself as the poor man's hunting dog, as I hail from the finest pedigree, but how could I argue, since I did not speak English or any other human language (although I could of course understand them perfectly well). So I barked.

I was told to keep quiet.

Once I was outside, a favorite habit of mine was running my mouth and nose along the pavement. I was always looking for food, never mind the two square meals a day I was guaranteed. At least in South Jersey, I found my breakfast, lunch, and dinner on the ground, but there were very slim pickings on Park Avenue, Seventy-Fourth and Seventy-Fifth Streets, and Lexington Avenue. Once I found half a bagel, which Mr. Rowley tried to take away from me. I had it fully in my mouth, though, and I knew he was afraid to put his hand in my mouth, as he thought I might bite him. Mrs. Rowley, who is of Hungarian heritage, as I mentioned, is more courageous and put her hand right in there when she was trying to stop me from swallowing something. One lady said, "A basset hound can smell a loaf of bread a block and a half away." I was never so lucky.

FLORA ROWLEY

I heard all about my predecessor from the Rowleys. Her name was Flora, and she was English, from Wittering in the county of Rutland. She, too, was a handsome basset and weighed five pounds more than me. She had the same colors and markings, although her white spots were larger. Perhaps I was her reincarnation? May she rest in peace up there.

Although I have never met a British dog, she must have barked with an English accent. I suppose the British have very good manners.

"She died of cancer of the leg," said Mr. Rowley, "It was all very sad, and I used to carry her down to the street."

Mrs. Rowley said, "Her ashes are beside my bed."

I hope I will live a long time.

The Rowleys had never owned a dog before Flora and certainly not one from a foreign country like England. As a child in Hungary, Mrs. Rowley and her sisters owned Ripi, a dachshund, but when they tried to escape from communist Hungary into Austria, they left Ripi behind, giving her to an aunt. The escape attempt failed, and the parents were put in prison, and Mrs. Rowley went to live with another aunt, but Ripi was no longer hers. As for Mr. Rowley, he had a cocker spaniel, but it was run over by an American Army truck in the street in front of his house in the English village where he lived during the Second World War.

When they got Flora, the Rowleys never wondered what kind of food was appropriate for a basset, so Flora was given the same food as they ate. I am much better behaved than Flora was regarding food, which happens to be my main interest in life. Flora would jump up on her hind legs and eat anything in sight—hot dogs, steak, toast, apples, cheese, and butter. Only if a plate of goodies is level with my mouth when I am standing on all fours will I make a grab for the delicacy, whatever it is. I am sure I will get brownie points in heaven, if not before, God willing. Flora will have to be reeducated in the next world—not me.

I remember the Rowleys said they bought Flora from a kennel in a village in the middle of England. She was one of about seven puppies flopping around on the concrete apron of the kennel in Wittering. Rutland is the smallest county in the United Kingdom. It was well-known for its fox hunts. I would have liked that, though I would have had a hard time keeping up with the hounds. Anyway, now they only run after a dragged scent since fox hunting was banned by the Brits. With my short legs, I still could not have kept up. It's a hard life being a basset hound.

Back to dear Flora's story. When the Rowleys looked over the seven puppies, Mr. Rowley liked one that had a beige and white coat—just like mine! Serendipity! Anyway, they put her in the hold of a 747 and flew her to New York. The shock of the transatlantic flight (there was little food and water, and it was freezing cold) nearly killed her, and she then caught some illness in upstate New York, which also nearly killed her. I guess British bassets are not as strong as American bassets.

On the delicate subject of bathroom habits, Mr. Rowley had remarked, "Flora was once naughty eight times in one day in our apartment!"

I never did No. 1 and No. 2 more than three times in a day in their Park Avenue apartment! That was over a period of twenty-four hours. I was not talking about my grand total of mishaps. Why did I call them mishaps anyway? Why should humans decide where dogs should go to the bathroom? A carpet was much more comfortable than the street, particularly for a female such as myself.

Mr. Rowley told me once that Flora broke loose on Seventy-Second Street and ran all the way to our building on Seventy-Fifth Street, dodging traffic.

"It looked like an English hunting scene. I tried to catch her, but every time I nearly caught up to her, she sped away."

Flora loved to chase the cats around the apartment, but whenever she was about to catch one, Tilly or Pokey would leap to the safety of a chair or table. Mr. Rowley, I am told, tried to stop Tilly from scratching the furniture by shooting at her with a water pistol, but despite getting wet, Tilly ignored him. Humans are so silly. If Tilly had been at the O'Dells, she could have scratched away to her heart's content since none of their furniture was antique, and it all came from Walmart. At any rate, I had nothing to do with Tilly's departure, which was six months before I arrived.

Mr. Rowley was English and clearly had not learned all of our American customs. He immigrated here when he was eleven in 1945.

He is telling my story for me, as I cannot read, write, or talk English, although I am much smarter and more observant than Mr. Rowley. I also have a much better sense of smell. For example, Mr. Rowley once said to a woman who was walking her dog while he exercised Flora, "I'm amazed how Americans spend thousands of dollars on medical care for their pets. When I was a child in England, we never bothered to take dogs to the vet. We just let them live or die."

The American lady said, "We do things differently here."

I am glad I am an American.

When Caroline and her friends were about eight years old, they used to dress Flora up in women's clothes. A bra was fastened around her chest, and she wore a skirt and scarf around her neck.

They attached clip-on earrings to her ears, but Flora shook them off. They tried putting Caroline's mother's stockings on her legs, but they always came off. Fortunately, Caroline was eighteen when I arrived and had outgrown the desire for humiliating my breed. I would never wear a bra or a skirt. What would other dogs think?

Once when the Rowleys took Flora up to their house in the northern Catskills, they introduced her to Lee, the taxi driver in Tannersville. Lee said, "That's the saddest looking dog I've ever seen." Lee must have been a very ignorant man. All bassets look sad. That's why we're so happy.

That summer, the Rowleys went to England for six weeks for business and pleasure. Tilly spent the summer in a cattery, and they must have mistreated her, because when she came back to 815, she refused to use the kitty litter box, preferring Mrs. Rowley's favorite oriental carpet. The Rowleys promptly found a friendly family on Long Island for her.

Of course, I never met Flora, though I knew I was her reincarnation. Poor Flora. Her last days were painful. While the Rowleys were in Europe on one of their trips, she was staying with a virtual stranger who finally took her to the vet after she had been limping for several days. Mrs. Rowley was very annoyed at him for taking so long about it. It was cancer.

As soon as the Rowleys returned, they took Flora to the Animal Medical Center in New York where they had to cut off part of the side of her left paw. They cut off some more three weeks later. Mr. Rowley used to carry her in his arms—all seventy pounds of her (minus a few ounces)—down the service elevator so she could do her business on the sidewalk.

Mr. Rowley, so he told me, wore a dirty old cashmere sweater to carry Flora downstairs. One weekend, some relatives of Mrs. Rowley's were visiting, and Mrs. Rowley said to Mr. Rowley, "Why do you have to wear such a dirty sweater?" As Mr. Rowley found Flora and her seventy pounds to be very heavy, and he considered himself a kind of Florence Nightingale hero to be carrying Flora around, he was quite annoyed.

Mr. Rowley wanted Flora to die a natural death, but Mrs. Rowley thought it would be more humane to put Flora to sleep. So on the appointed day, the vet, a young woman, came to the Rowleys' apartment. Not wanting to be present, Mr. Rowley went off to play tennis with a friend early that morning. Flora died in Mrs. Rowley's arms, and Mr. Rowley returned home just as the vet was leaving. He could see Mrs. Rowley on the couch holding Flora's body.

The pet mortician was supposed to arrive immediately afterward, but he did not turn up for an hour and a half. Mrs. Rowley held Flora during all that time. Finally, he arrived and took Flora away in a plastic bag. A day later, he returned Flora's ashes in a little container, and Mrs. Rowley now keeps the ashes in a secret hiding place near her side of the bed.

And so it was that the Rowleys decided to get a dog that looked just like their beloved Flora. Mrs. Rowley had a conversation with another basset hound devotee in Central Park, and through the Internet, she found my farm in South Jersey. And the rest, as they say, is history. *My* history.

YOU AIN'T NOTHING BUT A HOUND DOG

I noticed that disputes frequently broke out between Mr. and Mrs. Rowley over who should take me out so that I could perform my bathroom functions. I wanted to do my business four or five times every twenty-four hours, but not when I was sleeping, of course. For some reason, neither of them seemed to want to go outside with me, particularly at night or in the early morning. I liked the outdoors, because there I might see other dogs. Usually, Mrs. Rowley won these arguments.

I preferred to be with Mrs. Rowley, as she would get down on the floor and hug and kiss me, whereas Mr. Rowley stayed aloof, looking down upon me, being so British.

In the service elevator with me shortly after I arrived, Mr. Rowley liked to sing the first bars of Elvis Presley's *You Ain't Nothing but a Hound Dog*. He had a terrible voice. I already knew I was a hound dog from South Jersey. So the whole thing was unnecessary and very irritating, but my long, soft ears trailing on the ground blocked out some of his off-key voice. I suppose Mr. Rowley thought it was funny, but I didn't.

I heard that David Barford, one of my owner's English real estate agents, visited New York without contacting him. One day, he walked up Park (Shark) Avenue and couldn't help noticing how expensive and well-groomed the dogs were, representing a myriad of top breeds!

Generally speaking, I was resistant to being pulled by my neck to go down to the street. Would you want to be pulled by your neck whenever your boss wanted you to go to the toilet? I particularly objected to being outside when it was raining. I always got wet, and I noticed Mr. Rowley held the umbrella over his head but not over mine. I was also unhappy about umbrellas, and when I'd see the umbrella in his hand in the elevator, I shied away from it. It reminded me of when I'd been beaten by a stick on the O'Dell farmstead.

Shortly after I arrived on Park Avenue, I met the dog walker who had ten dogs. She was very tall and thin with uncombed hair, a baseball cap, sports jacket, and WASP features. I overheard someone say she had been a Park Avenue matron but had suffered brain damage after being kicked by a horse. Now she thinks she has no money and became a dog walker. I liked being independent instead of being pulled along with nine other dogs of all different sizes and shapes. And I never knew what kind of diseases they might have, so I did not try to sniff or bark at them. And these dogs are made to march in formation. Such regimentation would not suit me! Not one whit.

Sometimes, small dogs barked at me, but I never barked back. I knew I could eat them for lunch. Dachshunds and Chihuahuas would have been very tasty. But if an approaching dog were my size, it was a different story. Sometimes, I would charge at them until the leash stopped me. The best defense was offense. Dick Cheney would have agreed with me, but he shoots people, and I've never shot anyone, not even Texas lawyers.

A GIANT DOG NEXT DOOR

Next door to my home at 815 Park Avenue is an eleven-story townhouse that belonged to a famous musician. Just beyond the townhouse is a big apartment building made of what look like white bricks. One day, the biggest dog I ever saw in my life came out of there. It was a bullmastiff. I was fascinated but terrified. He had the biggest penis I've ever seen, and when he did No. 1, it was like a flood. Mrs. Rowley said I was sexually attracted to him. As only bassets can, the moment I saw him, I began to howl. Mr. Rowley said, "Sssh. Stop it! *Stop it*!" I tried to charge wildly at the 125-pound dog, but the leash held me back.

That dog paid no attention to me. It was as if I didn't exist. I bayed and bayed, but the mastiff walked along in his powerful, stately way. I don't know what would have happened if I had attacked the mastiff. I suppose it would have been the end of me. What a way to go! I kept on barking until the mastiff's owner, a doctor, took him back inside the white brick building. Mr. Rowley was becoming quite annoyed and kept telling me to be quiet. I kept up my howl until I got back inside 815. I never got the opportunity to either make love or fight him. I suppose Freudian psychoanalysts could have read something into my behavior.

Now let me tell you a story about Puff Daddy and Flora. I heard Mr. Rowley say that when Flora was alive, he went to Mass at St.

Jean's (that's the Roman Catholic church a block away on Lex) one Sunday, and the gospel was the one about Christ walking on water. So after Mass, Rowley shook hands with the pastor and said to him, "I have a neighbor who can walk on water." The priest looked surprised. So Mr. Rowley added, "My neighbor is Puff Daddy, the rock star, and he gave my daughter a photo of himself walking on water." The clergyman laughed.

I did occasionally meet another basset hound on the street near where I lived or in Central Park, where I was taken to chase squirrels. But I never caught any. There were two bassets—Napoleon and Josephine—but they were very old and moved very slowly, even slower than me when I am not in the mood for fast travel. Then Napoleon died, and a few months later Josephine disappeared. So I figured she must have gone up to our basset heaven.

Shortly after my arrival on Park Avenue, I had been deeply insulted. Caroline was walking me one day, and she introduced me to Dr. James Reardon, a plastic surgeon, who has an office on Park. He said, "I could do a lot of work on her," meaning me. "Ears, eyes, a tummy tuck, and cellulite in those legs." However, most people think I'm beautiful, particularly women. They're always saying, "Isn't she cute?" and the like.

Once, a woman in a fur coat, a stranger, gushed to Mr. Rowley, "She's so beautiful."

I was shocked to hear him reply, "Well, we haven't turned her into a handbag yet." I noticed the woman was shocked, too.

One day, I was taken to a dog show by Letitia, my very own personal walker. I did not compete in the show, as I have been fixed, because you have to be a whole dog to be in a dog show, but I walked around, looking at the other dogs and their owners. To Letitia's surprise, though not to mine, the director of the video decided to place me as the star attraction at the beginning and then again at the end of the show. If I'd only had an agent, I could have charged them a fee. It was on PBS, Channel 13, here in New York City.

On another occasion, I was stopped by a Frenchman on the sidewalk who showed Letitia and me pictures of his *bassay*. Then, another time, a limousine pulled up right next to us. The chauffeur got out, went round the car, and opened the door. The male passenger stepped out, exclaiming, "I just love basset hounds!" He bent over and stroked me. "I simply had to say hello to your basset hound."

THE TOY STORE

I have strong views about who I like and dislike. My enemies are little girls, so I try to bite them, but Mr. and Mrs. Rowley or Caroline always hold me back. I hear them say, "That's all we need is to be sued."

There is something about their little plaid skirts and cute faces, always saying, "Mommy, is that a basset hound?" or "What kind of a dog is that, Mommy?" that annoys me no end.

I also loathe boys on skateboards, and on two separate occasions, I nearly caught one by the ankle when he came rushing by me, crashing his board into the sidewalk to show how clever and athletic he was. The noise frightened me. I got the feeling that Mr. Rowley, even though he held me back, kind of approved of my hatred of these brats. After all, I was a Park Avenue dog and expected boys to behave like gentlemen, even though I knew many of them were not. I don't think those boys went to the Buckley School, a fashionable day school down my Seventy-Fourth Street from Park, but maybe they were students there.

There were two psychiatrists in my building, but they both refused to treat me. One was Dr. Howard Bogard, who specialized in hypnosis therapy for smokers. I have never smoked cigarettes. I heard Mr. Rowley say to him, "Amelia is a very neurotic dog. She doesn't like little girls, boys on skateboards …" The doctor laughed, but I could tell he had no intention of taking me on as a patient. Not that it would have done any good, as I don't believe in psychiatry. Dogs existed long before Freud was a spark in his father's eye, and look what a beautiful specimen I evolved into without the benefit of long hours on a couch—though I do like to lie on the Rowleys' couch, which is more comfortable than the carpet or the two round dog beds I own, where I leave a goodly amount of fur.

I soon found out that shedding hairs caused problems for the Rowleys when they rented a car. Before they returned it to the rental agent, Mr. Rowley would borrow a brush from the doormen at 815 Park and try to remove my hairs so that he wouldn't be charged by the ever-alert employees of the car rental place on East Eightieth Street.

When I had just about ceased being a puppy and already weighed fifty-five pounds, I nearly died. This happened one night when Mr. Rowley was walking me along Seventy-Fifth Street, and we were just in front of our neighborhood synagogue, Temple Israel. I suddenly saw a delicious-looking red and green something on the ground. It looked so tasty. Darting at it, I immediately swallowed it. It was about one and a half inches in diameter and made of wool, rubber bands, and wire mesh. However, about half an hour after we got back to my apartment, I began to feel very ill and collapsed on the carpet while making loud, terrifying choking sounds. I couldn't move.

Mrs. Rowley said, panic in her voice, "What's wrong with Amelia?"

Mr. Rowley confessed, "I saw her eat what looked like one of those scrunchies that girls wear in their hair to hold their ponytails."

"She's going to die!"

Caroline said, "We'd better take her to the emergency room at the Animal Medical Center!"

Mrs. Rowley and Caroline got a taxi and took me to the hospital. This was about eleven at night, and the doctors and nurses made me swallow some stuff that made me throw up. By two in the morning, I was back in my apartment. In disgrace, Mr. Rowley had been left behind. He looked relieved when we walked back in. Because he had been so worried about me, I don't think he could fall asleep. At least I hope so.

It was just a matter of time before my beauty and independence of character would bring me fame. *The New York Times,* in its Metropolitan Diary of February 11, 2002, wrote, "Marian Miller was shopping for gifts for her dog-owner friends in Z Spot, the pet store of Zitomer's on Madison Avenue, when she noticed a huge, sad-eyed basset hound sniffing around all the baskets on the floor, testing the toys. 'Hurry up, Amelia,' the dog's owner urged, 'We don't have all day.'

"Amelia continued to pick up one stuffed toy after another, trying each before putting it back. Finally, she settled on a colorful ball and trotted off with it in her mouth. She was the center of attention, and her owner then informed the fascinated spectators that Amelia had a weekly allowance to come in and shop. The two-legged shoppers all had a good laugh."

The New York Times is usually a very accurate newspaper, but I should point out that it was not my owner, but my dog-walker, Letitia, who took me there. But then, between you and me, I think

MONDAY, FEBRUARY 11, 2002 THE NEW YORK TIMES **METRO**

Metropolitan Diary

Marian Miller was shopping for gifts for her dog-owner friends in Z Spot, the pet store of Zitomer's on Madison Avenue, when she noticed a

huge, sad-eyed basset hound sniffing around in all the baskets on the floor, testing the toys. "Hurry up, Amelia," the dog's owner urged. "We don't have all day."

Amelia continued to pick up one stuffed toy after another, trying each before putting it back. Finally, she settled on a colorful ball and trotted off with it in her mouth. She was the center of attention, and her owner then informed the fascinated spectators that Amelia had a weekly allowance to come in and shop. The two-legged shoppers all had a good laugh.

• • •

A NEW YORK VALENTINE

The New York Times says about me.

Letitia liked to say she was my owner. Who wouldn't? More about Letitia later.

Then Zitomer closed the Z store. However, nobody told me, or at least I didn't understand Letitia's Filipino accent. For weeks, I dragged Letitia, who doesn't weigh much more than me, in front of the storefront, yearning for an encore before my adoring public.

Soon thereafter, I heard Mrs. Rowley's wonderful suggestion to Mr. Rowley, "I want Amelia to sleep in our bed."

However, Mr. Rowley's reaction was, "I'm not having a sixty-five-pound basset hound sleeping between us!"

What does Mr. Rowley have against basset hounds? I would not have done No. 1 and No. 2 in the bed.

I dream on an oriental carpet.

However, I noticed a little later that Mrs. Rowley brought one of my round beds into their bedroom on the side of the bed where she slept. I like that, as I like being near Mrs. Rowley, although at four or five in the morning, I like to go back to the kitchen where I can move around. I get bored, and I do a lot of sleeping during the day anyway, as there is no one to play with. Remember that I was the one who drove away Pokey the cat, and the cockroaches are hardly companions. It's true that there have been times that I have misbehaved on the carpet beside the bed, and Mrs. Rowley has started putting down blue diapers and little white carpets on the floor around my round bed. She also put up a little gate so I couldn't escape from the bedroom at night.

PUFF DADDY

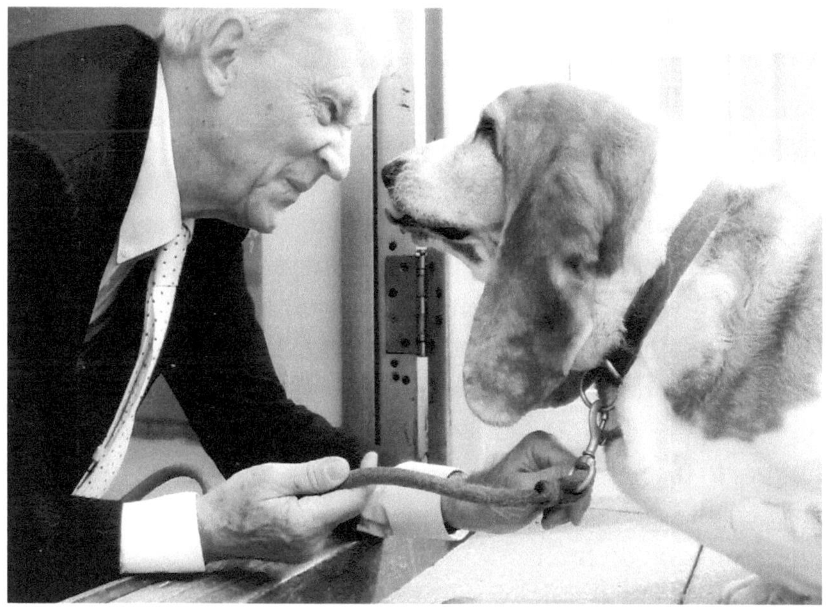

We miss Puff Daddy as a neighbor. Photo by Matthew Schaeffer.

Puff Daddy used to live next door to me. In case you didn't know, Puff is a famous rock promoter and rapper—more famous than me and definitely a tier-one celebrity, whereas I am not even tier five. I did not know then his real name was Sean Combs, but I did see Jennifer Lopez go in and out of his building. She was living with Puffy. Let me explain why it was Puffy's building. 813 Park was a townhouse with six stories added to the top of it. It was a rental—three expensive apartments of about three floors each, one on top of the other—three townhouses one on top of the other, as the rental agent described them on the billboard outside. The gossip was that Puffy had rented one of them and then bought the whole building. Also, I used to see Puff's baby from an earlier marriage being pushed in a baby carriage by a nurse wearing an immaculately starched uniform.

I know Caroline went to a concert of his at Madison Square Garden with some girlfriends when she was fifteen, and Mr. and Mrs. Rowley were very worried because they knew several people had been killed in a riot at one of Puffy's earlier concerts uptown. That was before Puffy moved into the neighborhood.

I am not prejudiced. In fact, I am politically correct as I am both brown and white. I suppose I could easily pass as an African-American dog in Africa except for my large white spots, but I am happy to live on Park Avenue, even though African-Americans are a rare sight among the residents around me. Perhaps I would have been more at home in Harlem, but the Rowleys were treating me well. I knew Puffy and his bodyguards delivered thousands of turkeys to the poor uptown at Thanksgiving. Indeed, I would have enjoyed all that turkey and stuffing if I'd only been living north of East Ninety-Sixth Street.

Puffy's bodyguards were very big, tall black men with wide necks, and I used to see them chatting and smoking when I came outside with Letitia or one of the Rowleys. I never bit any of their ankles as I'm not sure who would have won the fight. The bands Puffy managed traveled in a Winnebago that they parked in front of 813. I was with Mrs. Rowley one day when she and I approached their Winnebago, and Mrs. Rowley knocked on the middle door.

I heard her say to the large gentleman who opened the door, "Can I see inside?"

The person replied, "Lady, would you let me in your living room?"

I knew Mrs. Rowley did not approve of the Winnebago, which sometimes parked in front of 815, making it more difficult for the residents of 815 to go into our building when they got out of a taxi. Trucks and large vehicles are not allowed to park on Park unless they are actually loading and unloading.

Since Mrs. Rowley is one of the board members in charge of our building, she was therefore in a position to instruct the doorman on duty to call the police. A police car would arrive. Puffy's man would drive around the block and then park it where it had been before the police came. I once saw this happen three times during my hour's walk with Letitia.

However, on this occasion, Mrs. Rowley had walked into Puffy's lobby at 813 Park, and I heard her complaining again to one of the bodyguards about their parking habits.

Then a tough male voice said menacingly, "Lady, you're starting to annoy me." I could see through the corner of my left eye around one of my big ears that the bodyguard was about 6'4" and 250 pounds, while Mrs. Rowley is 5'8" and 135 pounds.

She retreated quickly from their lobby and came out onto the sidewalk.

I remember when Puffy was accused by the police of allegedly throwing a pistol out of his Lincoln Navigator after leaving a nightclub downtown with Jennifer. Life was quieter in front of 813 after that, and I saw several white men in coats and ties go in and out. I suppose they were lawyers. Jennifer moved out. I was sorry to see her go. She was almost as beautiful as me. Anyway, it all ended happily, and Puffy was acquitted. After that, Puffy changed his name to P. Diddy.

My next encounter with P. Diddy and his friends occurred one night when Mr. Rowley was walking me in front of 813. I did No. 2 on the sidewalk.

A beautiful young woman dressed to the nines wearing lots of makeup and carrying a Gucci handbag emerged from the front door.

She said sharply to Mr. Rowley, "Pick it up!"

I think of the boss as a stuffy old Englishman. He looked frightened, which is unusual for him.

He picked up my poo.

Another day, I saw P. Diddy crossing Park at Seventy-Fourth Street, wearing a stylish tan-colored woolen warm-up suit manufactured by Sean John. That was P. Diddy's clothing line. I'm told he sold two hundred million dollars worth of his outfits annually. Since my brown and white fur is so perfect, I've never bought one.

Then, P. Diddy or Sean Combs sold the building. I saw him in the lobby admiring his reflection in the mirror just before he moved out. I heard he moved to Alpine, New Jersey. Whoever heard of Alpine? But, then, whoever heard of Gibbsboro? I miss him, his bodyguards, and his bands. Park Avenue has never been so exciting, at least from a basset's viewpoint.

Mr. Rowley calls my name in that friendly superior voice that has a trace of English accent but is also American preppie. What else can you expect of an owner who lives in a sort of semipenthouse on Park Avenue? As I am lying there, reclining on my back, my legs wide open, revealing my most intimate parts, I open my eyelids long enough to stare at him. I do not deign to answer him, although if he offered me a cookie, I would respond. Back to sleep. I'll dream of Puff.

LETITIA

My next favorite person after Mrs. Rowley and Caroline is Letitia, my Filipino dog walker. When I first came to 815, she used to come in the kitchen door, crying, "Baby doll! Baby doll!" Mr. Rowley would wince. Then she realized such enthusiasm did not go over well on Park Avenue. So she toned down the volume of her greeting. I still wagged my tail happily and rushed toward her. She fell on her knees, hugging me. I licked her face. "Squirrels," she exclaimed happily, "Amelia, we're going to chase squirrels."

Who was Letitia? She came from the Philippines and had been married to an American lawyer. She used to be a real estate broker in Manhattan, but I heard her say shortly after I met her, "I prefer dogs to people." I love her dearly, though I would sometimes get embarrassed when I tripped over one of my ears when I was out with her. She was a pretty petite woman, and I was very upset when she had to go into the hospital for an operation. For two months, I had a male dog-walker. I prefer women as I am one, even though some stupid humans I encounter in the street refer to me as a male. Mr. Rowley always corrects them. This was usually during those conversations between Mr. Rowley and strangers about how cute I am. Really, I should have charged money for tickets to see me.

Perhaps I could have gotten rich and bought my own apartment on Park or Fifth and had Mrs. Rowley, Caroline, Letitia, and Mr. Rowley move in. I would have had my own maid service so that I wouldn't have had to go outside when I didn't want to. Basset heaven! As for food, the maids could open cans for me whenever I wished, as I cannot operate a can opener on account of my ears getting in the way.

I am always on the alert to protect Caroline.

GETTING OLDER

It was the spring of 2005, and I had turned five years old. By your human standards, that's seven times five, which makes me thirty-five—just old enough to run a hedge fund. I was becoming very disenchanted with the same old cans of dog food and the usual dog biscuits from D'Agostino's supermarket. So I started refusing to eat the glop that Mrs. Rowley would put in my bowl in the morning. This actually had a wondrous effect on Letitia and Mrs. Rowley. Letitia began to feed me hot dogs from the hot dog stand in Central Park. Since my trip up the Jersey Turnpike five years prior, I had learned that hot dogs are not made from dogs—or at least I hope not. And Mrs. Rowley would sometimes fry an egg and add it to my boring old dog food. Then Mrs. Rowley tried ham and Hungarian salami on me. I liked it.

However, that summer when the Rowleys took me up to their country house in the northern Catskills for the weekend, I started to throw up the ham and the salami. Some of it also came out of the other end of me in brown liquid form! It landed on the carpets in their Onteora Club house, although their carpets are pretty worn out compared to the oriental ones I love to decorate in their Park Avenue apartment! I noticed the furniture in their Onteora house was pretty run down compared to posh Park, but I had no control over the contents of either residence. Anyway, crisis was upon us!

Mrs. Rowley was giving a dinner party that night. Mr. and Mrs. Rowley telephoned the vet in New York, whom I do not like. It makes me very nervous when they drag me to the vet's office on Seventy-Sixth Street between Second and Third Avenues. Then Mr. Rowley offered to drive me to the Animal Emergency Medical Center in Kingston. Can you believe it? The road up the mountain by the big waterfall had caved in, so they had to drive me a longer way around, going down another mountain to Phoenicia. Of course, as soon we got there, I felt better. The doctor and a nurse pulled me by my leash onto a sort of board, which is a weighing machine. Sixty-five pounds! I could have told them that!

Then they left me in the hospital for the night. And they hooked me up to all kinds of tubes. The vet said, "Pancreatitis." I have no idea what that means … and I don't want to know. So much for Hungarian salami.

The next day, the vet said to Mr. Rowley, "Tell Mrs. Rowley if she wants to have a pet in the future, no more Hungarian salami!"

I quite agree. But it was delicious. Better than the American hot dogs I eat in Central Park. But then bassets have always been international. We have been described as English bassets, American bassets, and French bassets. All I know is that I am the reincarnation of Flora, who was English.

The next day, Caroline and Mr. and Mrs. Rowley came and collected me at nine in the evening as they were going to throw me out of the Kingston Emergency Center, which operates only weekends.

We were heading down the New York State Thruway, and I let out a terrific fart—silently. Soon the other passengers in the car were complaining.

Says Mrs. Rowley, "That's disgusting."

I cut another one.

More protests from the humans.

A cured basset, I returned to my Park Avenue apartment.

The next morning, I met a stocky, middle-aged man wearing a multicolored sports shirt who had a small, fluffy black dog. This canine tried sniffing my private parts. I first heard the expression *private parts* from Mr. Rowley who said he had first heard a British judge in a divorce trial referring to their *private parts* during oral sex between the estranged human couple. The sports shirt man said to Mr. Rowley, "Is she friendly?"

"Sometimes my dog is friendly, and sometimes she isn't."

The other man replied, "Like all of us."

As I am in a position to have my own private dog walker, I usually meet a higher class of dog, who like me, has only one human walker. I do not bark or sniff the lower class dogs who travel in packs led by a multiple walker.

Suddenly, I see the bullmastiff!! I bay. Or is it the full moon that excites me and not his enormous organ? Or am I just bored living alone in the Rowleys' apartment?

Puffy is gone, but I overhear Mr. Rowley chatting with one of the workmen renovating P. Diddy's former building. Why the new owner, an Italian-American, wants to tear up the inside of 813 and redo it is beyond me, as I had thought Puff's lifestyle next door was pretty luxurious. Anyway, this workman says, "We found several guns hidden in the walls underneath the floorboard."

Last night, a four-pound dog licked my nose just in front of the door at 815, and I snapped at it. Mr. Rowley said to Ramazan, "That'll teach little dogs to get close to Amelia."

I climb the step into the lobby. I look up at Gente, another doorman. Mr. Rowley gives him a little dog biscuit, and Gente, while I settle down on my haunches, gives it to me. Then Mr. Rowley hands another cookie to Steve, yet another doorman, who is Ramazan's son. Steve says, "That's my dinner." I do not think this is funny. He gives me the biscuit anyway.

Tonight, I attacked a slightly larger dog, a sort of Scottie, but Mr. Rowley held me back. I got two biscuits from Ramazan.

The next night, I heard two boys shouting from behind, "That's a basset hound. That's a basset hound." I paid no attention and walked into our building. The door closed behind me, and these two eight-year-olds or whatever they were, ran up to the door, repeating what I already know. Yes, *I am* a basset hound.

One morning, I stared at my double reflection in the polished brass door and the sides of the service elevator, waiting for it to open so I could trot to our back door and then into the kitchen. This is, of course, where breakfast would be awaiting me if Mrs. Rowley had already prepared it. Otherwise, there was always my water bowl to drink from and then a happy canter around the apartment in search of Mrs. Rowley and my bed beside her. I love Mrs. Rowley very much since she hugs and kisses me and gets down on the carpet with me—a very sensual experience which only I, a basset hound, can truly appreciate.

However, one morning, Mrs. Rowley had not prepared my food. I could hear Mrs. Rowley and Mr. Rowley discussing where I might have hidden a No. 2 deposit in the living room. Obviously, I was not going to tell them where it is. Although they do not hit me like the O'Dells did, Mr. Rowley says harsh words to me like "bad dog, bad dog!" about my little accidents. With Bounty and cleaning fluid, Mrs. Rowley then gets down on the floor.

Speaking of close encounters, on Sunday, December 10, 2006, at eight in the morning, Mr. Rowley walked me around the corner of the building into Seventy-Fifth Street where I saw an attractive young woman with a pert face following a mongrel brown dog wearing a bright red jacket on a leash. As they passed me, I leapt forward, growling, but Mr. Rowley's leash held me back. Better luck next time!

A few weeks later, on a very cold winter night, I was at the corner of Seventy-Fifth and Park when a youngish middle-aged man wearing a dark business suit approached, holding two dogs, one of them a black cocker spaniel. The spaniel stuck its nose in my rear. I am used to this, but after a few seconds, I got annoyed and growled. The dog's owner said to Rowley, "I don't blame her. I wouldn't want my behind sniffed at."

One of the workmen in front of 823 Park, which is being renovated into very expensive co-ops, including one reportedly for Robert DeNiro for a reputed forty million dollars, said this afternoon in front of me, "That dog leads some life."

Letitia said, "And she doesn't even know she's a millionairess."

Tonight, two innocent little black Scotties came toward me, marching rapidly in unison. I charged at them, growling. That'll teach them. Do I need a psychiatrist? After they passed, I stared at them for a long time.

I miss Diddy and the bodyguards, but Mr. Rowley, who loves gossip, tells me they're still active. Apparently Puffy is having a romance with one Sienna Miller. Mr. Rowley says he read this in *The Sunday Times* of London. I think she used to be a girlfriend of Jude Law until he slept with their babysitter. Basset hounds have better morals than humans. I'm glad to hear this news of my former neighbors.

Last night, I heard Mr. Rowley say to Mrs. Rowley, "A mouse ran across the white carpet while I was watching television."

"Oh, no!"

Mrs. Rowley then complained, "Why doesn't Amelia catch them?"

I'm asleep most of the time. Why should I catch them?

I am very sensitive to my daughter's boyfriends, even new ones, especially at the beginning. I think of Caroline as my daughter, even though I know full well she is Boss Rowley's offspring and also that of my beloved Terez. Anyway, I heard Caroline tell her father to go into his office.

"Stay out of sight," she said. "----'s coming."

I knew Mrs. Rowley had already been banished to their bedroom. Then he came in, and I went bananas. I started crying and wagging my tail like I do when Mrs. Rowley comes back from a trip and I haven't seen her for a long time.

This new boy was so tall and handsome. I had to crane my neck to be able to see him, dark hair and all. Probably works for a hedge fund. I could tell Caroline likes him. He had a low, gravelly voice. I was whining, crying, wagging my tail, and swiveling my body. Ah, love. I went back to sleep. Then they went away in the elevator.

Later that evening, Mrs. Rowley showed Mr. Rowley a photo of Caroline and "----." It showed him in a dinner jacket and Caroline leaning against him, looking very beautiful. In South Jeersey (sic), we call dinner jackets tuxedos.

How I see Caroline Rowley.

DAILY LIFE

Because Mr. Rowley has refused to let me sleep on the double bed between them, I awake about six on the little round bed beside Mrs. Rowley. She is just above me. If I'm lucky or wag my tail vigorously enough to make a noise, Mrs. Rowley staggers out of bed in her nightgown and takes me down to the kitchen where I'm locked in by a movable gate on one side of the kitchen and a door at the other entrance. The Rowleys know I don't like to do my business in a confined space like the kitchen. Although I don't mind padding through other dogs' No. 1 outside, indoors I would have to smell it, or, God forbid, walk in it.

However, Mrs. Rowley does not wake up this Saturday morning, and it's not until Mr. Rowley rolls out of his side of the bed at about seven and hears my tail wagging that he leads me out of the bedroom and into the kitchen. I notice he fails to close the door fully behind him.

Then he makes coffee with hot milk and squeezes a fresh orange for juice for himself without offering me any. He goes out to the living room and sits by the window overlooking Temple Israel and the east side, drinking his coffee and thinking great thoughts. I surreptitiously push open the door and pad through his office, down the little hall, and emerge near the great man. Then he sees me. "Amelia, get back into the kitchen." I cooperate. After a while, he comes into the kitchen again—fully dressed—and takes me outside. On returning, I am offered my bowl of dog food, but I decide to ignore it, at least for a half-hour or so.

The night before, as Mr. Rowley had been walking me back to our building, two young men, dressed almost entirely in black, one of them smoking a cigarette and wearing sports shirt and trousers, had passed me by. I don't like the color black, and I had leapt at them. As Mr. Rowley's leash held me back before I could sink my teeth into a black trouser leg, I heard one of them say with a sarcastic laugh, "Friendly dog."

The very next morning, a nice woman approached Mr. Rowley and me, saying "Good morning." She had a black dog with her, about the same size as me. When the mutt got near, I snapped at her—the dog, I mean.

Another time, Mr. Rowley, sometimes jokingly referred to by his friends in his tennis club as Lord Peter, encountered one Jim Neff, a tall somewhat elderly man with a wide friendly smile. I was doing No. 1 a few feet from the front of 815. Looking up from my vantage point a little above the cuffs of his trousers, I could see he was wearing a Central Park Conservancy sweatshirt, identifying him as one of the many volunteers who keep the park in tip-top shape. Jim said, "You should take Amelia to Central Park before nine when dogs are allowed to be off their leash."

I was hoping Mr. Rowley would take Jim's cue and take me there.

"But there are three thousand dogs running loose, and all you hear are cries of 'Louise … Bonzo … Fido.'"

In the meantime, I had been sniffing Mr. Neff's shoes.

He suddenly says, "I have the blood of squirrels on them."

Rowley jokingly says to Neff, "You murdered the squirrels."

Back at the apartment, I am feeling ashamed. An hour earlier,

I had deposited several "sausages" on the dining room carpet beneath the oil painting of an Argentine house—a very small one, more the size of a shed, somewhere out in the middle of nowhere, perhaps the Pampas. Sometime later, Mr. Rowley, having finished his dinner in front of the TV set in the adjoining "new" room, notices my No. 2. It is time to take me out.

The next morning, Mr. Rowley gently kicks my sleeping bed shaped like a circle. I bark at him, thrusting my jaws threateningly toward him. He jumps back. This incident reminded me of being kicked as a puppy by my breeders, the O'Dells, at the Jersey dump in order to try to make me move faster.

Then we go downstairs using the service elevator.

The Rowleys have a rambling old house in the mountains where I accompany them for a change of air and scenery. Early one morning in May, Lord Rowley, as I occasionally refer laughingly to my master, in order to buy a newspaper, decides to take me with him in his SUV to the town of Tannersville, New York, known as the Paris of the Catskills. He pulls me by my neck to the open side door. That SUV is very high off the ground! I have a long rocketlike body. I cannot jump up to the floor of the vehicle. Rowley lifts my front paws onto the car floor. Then he puts his arms under my hips. He heaves. I scrape my rear legs on the edge of the SUV floor, and I am inside. Life is not easy. Perhaps I should eat less or do Pilates or tai chi.

After our exhausting three-hour trip back to New York City from the Catskills, I spend most of the day sleeping. At nine-thirty in the evening, Mr. Rowley drags me across the street, but first he stops by Steve, the big tall doorman.

"Whose stuff is all that?" I hear him say. There are several bags and a bottle of wine.

"11 B," replies Steve. It means nothing to me but seems to

interest Boss Rowley. Across the street, he mails a letter. Then he walks me down to Seventy-Fourth, and we cross Park. Then a lady comes up with a furry medium-sized dog. I notice Boss Rowley holds me tightly by the leash. The furry creature sniffs my behind.

"Is that Amelia?" says the young woman, allowing her furry thing to sniff around me. "I've been telling my husband about her. She's beautiful. She's usually with a woman."

"That's Letitia," says the boss.

The furry animal's getting on my nerves. I snap at its nose.

"Sorry," says my owner.

The young woman pulls away, surprised.

Then we return to 815, and I hear Steve tell Mr. Rowley the name of the party in 11 B to whom the bags belong.

"It's a bottle of wine?" says Mr. Rowley, peering at it while holding me.

"Zinfandel," says Steve.

I'm standing there, waiting to be fed by Steve and Gente, the other doorman. Mr. Rowley hands each of them one of my cookies. I look from Steve to Gente, not knowing which to take. I swallow the one in Gente's fingers.

Steve looks at his.

"It's better than some food I've had. I once ate a goldfish."

My ears perk up.

Boss Rowley looks at Steve.

He smiles. "It was high school stuff."

I eat Steve's cookie.

Another boring day on Park Avenue. Time to go to bed next to Mrs. Rowley. I run down the hall, my tail wagging. She's my favorite friend. Back to sleep.

The next morning, I am doing my business by a yellow boxlike car. Mr. Rowley has trouble picking it up, as it's all crumbly, with his bag. Mr. Rowley walks toward the wastebasket at Seventy-Fourth and Park, holding my bag, dragging me along.

I hear a voice behind us.

"Peter, is that your lunch?" It's the Central Park Conservancy man, Jim Neff.

He strides purposefully past us.

Mr. Rowley shouts after him, "Would you like it?"

I like to sniff the flowers around the trees. There are pretty pansies and daisies, and sometimes, the earth inside the little fence smells good. Who knows? I might find something good to eat.

This morning, I saw a huge white fluffy dog across Seventy-Fourth Street. I decided not to let out my howl like I did when I saw the 125-pound bullmastiff.

Back in the apartment, I heard Mr. Rowley say to his wife, "The philosopher William James wondered what his dog must be thinking watching him reading books for hours on end and not moving a toe." Speaking of which, why *does* Mr. Rowley spend so much time staring at books and newspapers? He should be paying attention to me, the world's best basset hound. He sits absolutely motionless. I even see him staring at a screen on a computer or at a TV set.

Very odd. Bassets certainly know how to spend their time better, especially when they see someone of the opposite sex.

Then I heard him say to Mrs. Rowley, "William James was the brother of Henry James."

Who exactly was this William James? Who was Henry James? I let out a bark then, which I do very rarely.

I was disappointed to have to return home today. Robert had been my caretaker for a few days out in Queens; he's a plump jolly man. The hated Rowleys had gone off for one of their fashionable weekends to Locust Valley: "Low-Cost Valley," I heard Mr. Rowley say, thinking himself terribly witty. Anyway, Robert brought me back at seven-thirty, and Mr. Rowley let me in the back door. Then Mr. Rowley called to Robert, who'd gone back toward the service elevator. Robert came back into the kitchen, and I wagged my tail happily. I thought Robert was going to take me away again. No such luck!

Mr. Rowley said, "How much Clavamox?"

"Two pills a day."

I have a cystitis problem. As I'm a lady Park Avenue dog, I won't explain what that is. But down in South Jersey, the O'Dells used to say, "Ev'ry fuckin' quarthower peein' 'n pissin."

A new handler, Susie, comes into my life. Susie Moore. She helps Mrs. Rowley with her bills and other matters like parties and buying the penthouse above. Mrs. Rowley persuades her to take me out.

"That Letitia's on jury duty," Mr. Rowley says.

Mrs. Rowley tells him, "Letitia's been put on a case."

Susie brings me back in to the kitchen after our sojourn outside. Susie, who is half the height of Mr. Rowley, says emphatically, "She's a strong dog."

Of course I'm strong. I have to drag these humans around whenever I go outside.

I see piles of Mrs. Rowley's clothes in the living room—a bad sign. I start to cry. They must be going away.

I'm now living in Queens at the home of Jay, another doorman from 815 Park. Does Mrs. Rowley miss me? Does Boss Rowley? And Caroline? My transatlantic ESP tells me Mrs. Rowley cries at night and that she misses me. Basset hounds are very sensitive.

The Rowleys have returned. Lord Rowley takes me down the service elevator at six-forty-five this morning—too early! I had been sleeping peacefully beside Mrs. Rowley. It stops on the fifth floor, and I see a woman with wet hair and a Scottie. "I'll pick him up," she says. She obviously didn't want me to attack her pet. The boss says to the middle-aged woman with the wet blonde hair, "What's his name?"

She replies, "Anderson Cooper."

It's been really hot the last couple of days. As a basset hound, I don't like it. My tail drags outside, and I move slowly. And believe me, I can move slowly. I haven't felt like eating. Early this morning, Mr. Rowley was nicer to me than usual when he took me down in the service elevator, stroking my chin with its floppy folds and my long ears. What was going on, I wondered? Were they going away, and he felt guilty?

Yesterday, I didn't eat any of my canned dog food. It just sat there, and I ignored it. Even Letitia couldn't make me eat it. But this morning at about ten o'clock, I was *very* hungry. I could have eaten a horse or another basset hound. So I padded into Mr. Rowley's office, where he was sitting doing something useless, looking at some papers, and I thrust my head up by his knee and touched it. I've never done that before, but hunger drove me to it.

He got the message!

He got up and opened a can of dog food, put it in my bowl, and dropped it six inches onto the little carpet in the kitchen, where my food and water are kept. I ate it quickly. I'm one happy hound dog. Then I went to sleep on the oriental carpet.

I often like to climb under a Mark Hotel imitation Chinese cabinet and curl up. Mrs. Rowley had bought a lot of furniture from a sale at the Mark Hotel on Seventy-Seventh Street. The legs protect me from the Rowleys or Letitia putting a leash around my neck and suddenly pulling me out.

I heard Mr. Rowley recount to Mrs. Rowley a conversation he had had with Doug Warwick at the Union Club roundtable lunch today: "Mr. Warwick's mother raised basset hounds for pleasure, giving them away to friends. She had as many as thirty-five in all, and it was always painful when one died. The best-behaved ones were allowed in the house, but they were usually kept in kennels and allowed to run around in an enclosed field. She and her children trained them to sit, balance something on their nose, lie down, chase a ball, etc. But the dogs were always stubborn about obeying immediately, and Doug's family would try to guess how many seconds it would take for the pet to obey. One would say seven seconds, another two seconds, and Doug would say four seconds. Her dogs were not neutered, and she used only the best ones in shows."

Then Mr. Rowley offered, "Amelia takes her time obeying me in the service elevator when I tell her to sit. Sometimes, she doesn't sit at all. Then I have to push her rear end to sit down. This is when someone else gets on the elevator. They are afraid she'll bite them."

I admit I get nervous when I think or hear that the Rowleys are going to take one of their trips. What will happen to me? Who will take care of me? Of course, a lot of the time, I take care of the Rowleys, attacking dogs who might injure Mrs. Rowley, Caroline, or Mr. Rowley; frightening cockroaches and mice; and scaring bad men who might snatch Caroline's or Mrs. Rowley's handbags.

Now I hear the Rowleys are going to send Letitia in a car service twice a week to Jay's house in Bayside, Queens, while I am living there when they're in Europe. This is so I feel less lonely and still connected to my favorite family. I overheard that Letitia will take me for a walk for an hour in the streets of Queens near Jay's house. It sounds exciting, and I may make some new friends among the dogs out there. Of course, most of my friends these days are Park and Fifth Avenue dogs, but Queens canines are just as good as Manhattan ones. Life is certainly very different from when I was on the O'Dell farmstead in South Jersey.

Jay has been my favorite doorman ever since I moved in to 815 Park. Jay also liked Flora, my predecessor, which I know for a fact since I heard him say to Mr. Rowley that Flora was a very nice dog.

Summertime was upon us, and it was off to the Hamptons. I was resting on the beach in Southampton in front of the beach club, whose formal name is the Bathing Corporation of Southampton. It was eighty-five in the shade. Of course, I was under an umbrella. I didn't mind the feel of the sand in my fur and between my strong, thick toenails. I could hear the waves crashing on the sand. Then I heard a conversation between Mr. Rowley and a man and woman in their mid-thirties. They were talking about a little brown mongrel dog. I could see the animal. He was small and brown. He was cute. He had a little upturned nose, and he was running back and forth, sometimes in circles. He turned out to be owned by Alexandra Rowley, a very distant relation of my Rowleys. The little mutt was adopted by Alexandra and her husband from the Humane Society in New York and had severe anxiety attacks when his owners would go away. So now they give him a calming drug.

Nobody gives me tranquilizers when I get separation anxiety. Like the other day, I see this big black duffel bag stuffed to the zippers. Are they all going away *without me?* I whine and whine and cry. Basset hounds can be quite noisy when they cry. Mr. Rowley, who is unpredictable when it comes to sympathy, calls me, "Amelia … Amelia." Then he strokes me and caresses my neck and back. He even got down on the floor and gave me a hug. What's going on? That went on for about fifteen minutes. Eventually, I felt more secure. They still loved me. Finally, I stopped my euphonious crying when I understood that only Caroline's suitcase was packed, which meant that my boss and his wife were not going anywhere.

By the way, the beach club is exclusive. In fact, they won't even let me walk through its red-brick terrace and clubhouse, and Mr.

Rowley has to bring me round to the beach in front of the club by entering through a public car park.

It was now back to Queens.

My visit with Jay; his mother; his wife; her daughter, Camille, age seven; and their small dog began. I played in the garden with their pet. I liked the dry dog food their small dog ate and tried to eat it myself, which their animal didn't like. Then Jay mixed some of it into my food, and I was an even happier basset hound. I went on a camping trip. I heard I might be attacked by a bear. Would I have charged him, or would I have fled?

This morning, I returned to the Rowleys. I found Mr. Rowley and settled my long body beside his legs. He was wearing red trousers. My separation anxieties were over!

Early this morning, he had taken me downstairs in the service elevator, and I had padded out the front door past Jay, who had been guarding our building all night. Jay exclaimed enthusiastically, "*Amelia,*" but I ignored him as I had business to do outside. I heard Mr. Rowley say to Jay, "She'll say 'hello' when we come back." On my return, Jay gave me a big hug. Then, half an hour later, Jay came up to my apartment, and I nuzzled his legs.

This morning, I walked down the marble-floored lobby, and because it's fall (it's after Labor Day), the building now provides oriental carpets for my comfort. They are soft under my white paws. I saw Jay spraying the sidewalk with water in front of my building. When he saw me, he exclaimed, "*Amelia!*" I went bananas, wagging my tail, swiveling my body, squealing as only I can, and he gave me a big hug.

As I passed by, I saw Anthony, an African-American doorman, one of the very few on Park Avenue. He is about twenty-one years old. Anthony, I know, lives across the street, which is also very unusual for a Park Avenue doorman, as they all live in places like Queens, Brooklyn, or Staten Island. But I had heard Mrs. Rowley tell Mr. Rowley that Anthony's father is the superintendent of the building on the other side of the street. Mrs. Rowley had said to Mr. Rowley, "There was some surprise on the subcommittee of our board who interview new doormen when Anthony had said where he lived."

Anyway, I reach the corner of Seventy-Fourth Street and Park Avenue when Mr. Rowley suddenly stops as if he had been shocked. I looked down Seventy-Fourth, and there was this thin stunning creature with sensational legs in a tight black dress—a human female. She walks up to Mr. Rowley and says, "I'm D------." There then followed a conversation between my boss and the bombshell.

Then I went back to our entrance. Mr. Rowley said to Anthony, "Who was the young man by the entrance?"

"My brother. He wanted to borrow some money."

"Did you give him any?"

"Yes. It's the first day of school. Why not?"

An hour later, Mr. Rowley tells Caroline of his encounter with the sexy model, although Mr. Rowley did not describe her as such. It turned out D------ was a friend of Caroline's.

"Why," says Mr. Rowley to Caroline, "was D------ walking up Seventy-Fourth dressed to the nines at seven in the morning?"

Caroline replies, "She had spent the night with E------ and was going back to her apartment. The walk of shame."

Another morning about eight, Mr. Rowley takes me out, and I see several other small and large dogs. As a reward for each of my toilet exertions, I get to eat two tiny cookies. Before giving me two more cookies in the elevator, Mr. Rowley makes me sit on my haunches. Inside the apartment, I retreat to the living room, and I hear the muffled thud of my food bowl hitting the little carpet in the kitchen. I am not hungry. Then, when Mr. Rowley sits down with his breakfast tray by a window looking east above Temple Israel, I saunter out to where the sunlight streams onto a carpet and the parquet floor. Near Mr. Rowley's legs, I stretch out and enjoy getting a suntan, though since my fur is mostly brown, it will not change color. I like the sun, but after a while, I get tired of the hot rays and retreat back to my circular bed, where I lie down for a snooze, my chin on the raised round arm. Then I assume my new position of lying flat on my back with my legs suspended in air, my private parts fully exposed. Thus another morning starts, and in an hour or so, Letitia will arrive, allowing me an hour's excitement pursuing squirrels and dogs in the park.

I saw Mr. Rowley hand one of my cookies to Gente and another to Ramazan, our oldest doorman. But I prefer Ramazan to Gente, as I've known Ramazan a long time, though Gente is a very nice man. So I refused to eat the cookie Gente offered me and instead turned to Ramazan and ate the one from his hand. Then I swallowed Gente's, while Ramazan said, "We can see who Amelia likes more." Gente then started to fondle my neck and ears.

Upstairs, I did No. 1 beside the Rowleys' bed as Mr. Rowley had hurried me, because it was raining slightly, and I only had time to do one No. 1 and one No. 2. Mr. Rowley gave me a dirty look.

I had gone wild earlier this morning at seven-fifteen when I came out of the rear kitchen door, my neck trapped by Mr. Rowley's leash as usual (though I noticed recently that he has sometimes let me walk out without the leash to the service elevator door when I know he has to put it on me because the building says so. On very rare occasions, he lets me ride almost the whole way down the shaft before attaching it).

I wagged my tail and sniffed along the linoleum in front of the elevator. I realized my beloved doorman Jay had been on the fifteenth floor only a few minutes before. I even did a bit of sniffing inside the elevator after it arrived, and sure enough, when I came out on Park Avenue and turned right in order to do my business, there was Jay brushing the leaves on the corner of Seventy-Fifth Street. I rushed up to Jay, squealing, and received a hug and pat until Mr. Rowley said, "Come on, Amelia, Jay has to work."

What a great start to the morning! On the way back, when Mr. Rowley took me south on Park, I ran into a funny-looking brown dog with scraggly hair, smaller than me. Mr. Rowley held me tightly by the leash with his other hand.

The attractive young woman with the brown dog said, "My dog is not always friendly." We were starting to sniff each other's noses.

"Mine can be temperamental," I heard Boss Rowley say.

The young lady said, "They have the same color of brown." My coat is slightly darker, smoother, and more beautiful.

Mr. Rowley replied diplomatically, "The colors are similar. What kind of dog is yours?"

"A cockerpoo."

"A what?" said Mr. Rowley.

"Half cocker spaniel, half poodle." The other dog and I were pulled apart. I let out a snarl.

The Rowleys went away for a few days to the Caribbean—in a private jet! Why didn't they take me?

But I stayed a few days with a very friendly family in Queens and came home today. Milady, the sweet young Puerto Rican woman, one of my two caretakers, brought me up the service elevator at seven-thirty, a bit early, even for an adventurous basset like me.

I walked in the back door and saw all the Rowleys. The musky smell of my unwashed fur and skin floated up to them. But no matter. I am back, and they are glad.

"She needs a bath," I hear Mr. Rowley say. So what else is new?

"I agree," says a Hungarian-accented voice.

"Amelia," croons Caroline.

I wag my tail. Soon Mrs. Rowley is on the floor in her white nightgown, and I am snuggling up to her.

I notice, as more years pass and the memories of my early days with the O'Dells in South Jersey grow dim, that I express myself with more whines, squeals, occasional barks, and lots of wags. Are the Rowleys and I bonding? Is my full basset hound character emerging? When I see Jay, my beloved doorman, my squeals grow in frequency. It's a long way from South Jersey to Park Avenue. Or is it?

Last night, Mrs. Rowley gave me two new beds, and I am allowed to keep my old comfortable one with its faded blue color and soft encircling arm where I lay my head and tail after exercise and at night and when I am just plain bored. But this new round bed has a golden reddish brown hue and is even thicker than my regular one. It looks like it's made from velvet. It's luxurious and caressing to my basset hound body. I heard Mr. Rowley say, "I wish that were my bed."

Anyway, much to my surprise early this morning, Mr. Rowley takes me west on Seventy-Fifth Street toward Central Park instead of the usual short walk near the building. I stop as much as possible, sniffing the leaves. I smell the cold early December air and hear the sounds of the traffic and the footsteps of the parents and children going to school. I pass Carolina Herrera. Flora had once been taken in there when it was Givenchy, and she had done something unspeakable on their carpet, causing the shop ladies to scream in horror. Flora and Mr. Rowley had fled.

Mr. Rowley walks me up Fifth Avenue, and I enter the park opposite Seventy-Seventh Street. He sighs, "I used to bring Caroline here when she was little." We're beside the James Michael Levin playground. Michael was a boy who died when his head was crushed by a seesaw twenty-two years ago, and his parents built the playground in his memory. I am not allowed to go in it. Anyway, the gates are locked.

Then we encounter a pretty lady wearing a jacket and a soft hat. At the end of her leashes are two small black-and-white dogs. We're standing near the Alice in Wonderland statue.

"What are those?" says my owner.

"Japanese chin," she replies with a flirtatious smile.

"C - H - I - N?" asks Rowley coolly.

"Yes. We had two basset hounds, but we gave them to friends in upstate New York."

"How long did they live?"

"Sixteen years."

I knew that meant 112.

Then we left the park, walked east on Seventy-Second, and turned left onto Madison. Mr. Rowley started to walk faster. Why was he moving quickly?

At Seventy-Third Street, Mr. Rowley called out loudly, "Bob?"

Bob, who was wearing a warm-up suit, turned around. He has a club foot.

"Are you going to work?"

"Yup."

Then Bob made a joke about President Bush, "The first burning bush was in the Bible."

Bob entered a store where he is in charge of the counter selling men's toiletries.

Then we went home.

This morning, Mr. Rowley walked me to the park again. It was snowing. I saw a dozen or so sparrows huddling on a stone ledge. However, I was wearing my green jacket. This time Mr. Rowley let me off the leash, and I played with a wolfhound and a Labrador retriever.

One evening about nine forty-five, for reasons unknown to me and certainly to Peter Rowley, a medium-sized dog with middle-aged male owner approached us along Park. They were heading south, walking close to the buildings. I was on my red leash walking north near the street. For some reason, Peter put the fingers of his free hand, the right one, around the middle of the leash cord. I noticed the other dog, which had been on the street side of its owner, suddenly slip behind the man and then walk between him and the wall. As we passed them, I leapt at the impudent interloper, snarling and barking, but fortunately for the other dog, Mr. Rowley managed to restrain me.

The things people say! How insulting! There was this quite pretty Japanese woman with a slightly crooked smile and good teeth who had two dogs on leashes—a shaggy furry one and another (I don't remember what kind). She says sweetly to Peter, referring to me, "She's so obstinate!" What a word. Her English is very good.

Peter replied, "That's her breed."

As Mr. Rowley put the collar around my neck to persuade me to go downstairs this early sunny morning on St. Patrick's Day, he said, "Come on, you pampered Park Avenue dog."

Mr. Rowley photographed me sleeping, lying on my back with my legs wide open, once again exposing my most intimate areas to public view. Even though I appear to be asleep, I'm really not!

Yikes! Yesterday, Letitia and Avra, my vet, took me to a place I'd never seen before. I was too trusting. I should have known better. It was an animal hospital, and I hate animal hospitals. If it had been the Animal Medical Emergency Center, which I know all too well, I would have resisted with every muscle in my body. But it was too late. I was trapped. It is true enough that I have a toothache—and have had it for some months—on the lower left. I was hoping it would go away.

The next thing I knew, I found myself waking up as groggy as can be with a red bandage around my lower left ankle. I had to walk unsteadily to a taxi, and Letitia took me home where I sank into a deep sleep in my favorite red bed. No food and no water, but I didn't want any. Then around eight-thirty, I felt Mr. Rowley trying to lift the edge of my bed so that I would roll over to my other side and he could take off my bandage, but I gave him a little growl. He gave up.

The next morning I woke up and I still had a toothache, but it was much less painful. It was then that I realized there was a big gap in my lower left jaw. I vaguely remembered hearing the night before Mr. Rowley saying to Mrs. Rowley, "Letitia left us the tooth. It's big and red. Do you want to see it?"

Mrs. Rowley said, "Ugh. No way. Throw it out." My tooth! I hope they will give me a molar implant.

By eleven the next morning, I was feeling better and raised my head to survey the familiar scene of our living room. Nothing had changed. Though I usually spend the night on the floor next to my beloved Mrs. Rowley, I could see that I was still in the living room surrounded by an unusual circle of chairs, white rugs (these I recognized from the bedroom), wooden gates, and my water bowl on top of a white rug. What was going on? Had they left me there for the night because of my wounded condition?

Letitia arrived and removed my bandage. Perhaps Mr. and Mrs. Rowley had been afraid to, but I was just as glad not to have been bothered. Then I walked into the kitchen, and Letitia fed me my dinner by hand. You might think this was a special favor due to my operation, but in fact for some weeks previously, I had trained Letitia to feed me by hand, which is much more pleasant than having to lean down and eat it from a bowl. Then I went outside—minus my molar!

Surprise! I encountered two King Charles spaniels who had the same brown and white coloring as me. We touched each other's noses. I liked them. Their owner, a middle-aged attractive lady, said to Mr. Rowley, "What a pretty dog you have."

He replied, "You have pretty dogs, too."

More Park Avenue adventure. The great-grandson of Sacheverell Sitwell (Edith, Osbert, and Sacheverell were the famous Sitwell siblings), Bertie, an energetic twelve-year-old, came to see me yesterday. Letitia had said, "Amelia doesn't like a lot of children—noisy, screaming brats."

However, Bertie stroked my ears, and because he was gentle and respectful, I allowed him to take me on the elevator. Mrs. Rowley had forgotten to give Bertie my leash and warn him that I was not allowed to roam freely on the Park Avenue sidewalk and street. She thought Bertie was only going to take me one flight down from the new penthouse to my apartment. Bertie let me go alone in the elevator.

Soon I found myself on the ground floor as free as a bird. Perhaps there is a basset hound bird who flies by flapping her ears, though I have not met her yet. Instead of heading for the open front door, I waited by the C line lift (I call it that because Bertie is English and would not understand the word *elevator*, and of course Flora was English, whereas I am 100 percent American and proud to be from South Jersey).

Mr. Rowley suddenly appeared, flustered and holding my leash, and I was sent back upstairs, none the worse for wear. Later, I heard Letitia say after Mr. Rowley had told her of my adventure with this descendant of a famous literary family, "Did you know Amelia is a racist? The other day this sweet gay guy, who was black, came up to Amelia—his hands open—to hug her, and she backed away. I was embarrassed and lied that she was not feeling well."

Mr. Rowley said, "She doesn't like black dogs either." So it goes.

Back to my usual tricks! Nobody pushes a basset hound around, particularly when she has to go to the bathroom. Letitia failed to appear at four yesterday afternoon, and by four-thirty, I relieved myself on Mrs. Rowley's favorite oriental carpet. Letitia had not phoned to explain her absence, which was that Verizon was charging her three times what it was supposed to and that she had been therefore delayed at the Verizon office, arguing with an employee, as she later told Mr. Rowley, who then started to tell Mrs. Rowley, who exclaimed, "I don't want to hear it. She didn't have to clean it up." I noticed the carpet was halfway rolled up and the furniture moved. As I said, nobody pushes me around. And my gift to the Rowleys was a flood—more than usual!

Happy Day! I was lying on the carpet in the dining room watching John Pieza, Mrs. Rowley's computer consultant, and Susie, Mrs. Rowley's secretary, work at the table. Carmen, our part-time maid, was dusting a picture. The phone rang. John answered, spoke to Mrs. Rowley, who was at our house in England, and then held the receiver to my ear. In her unmistakable Hungarian accent, Mrs. Rowley said, "Darling. Darling. Darling. My Precious One. Precious One. I love you. I love you. I love you." My tail wagged and wagged.

One day, I was lying on the oriental carpeted floor by the front door. My instinct told me something exciting might be about to happen. Everyone was out—or at least Mrs. Rowley and Caroline. I hadn't seen Mr. Rowley for over a week. Mrs. Rowley had returned the day before from England. Then the elevator door opened and who should appear but Mr. Rowley carrying a briefcase and an orange-colored bag marked NBAA (that means National Business Aircraft Association). I was so happy. I wagged my tail, and Mr. Rowley leaned down and stroked my back several times. Such affection. Even though I knew he had been in England again, perhaps Mr. Rowley was becoming less English in manner.

I am supposed to be supervising the wildlife in our apartment. After all, I am much bigger than the mice and cockroaches who live in the walls and ceilings around me, and since I drove away Pokey the cat by barking at her after I arrived at 815 Park seven years ago, my job, I suppose, is to attack, catch, and kill the mice. But something has gone wrong with the plan because I heard Mr. Rowley complain the other day, "I was watching television, and a mouse ran right in front of me!"

Later on, I heard Mr. Rowley tell Mrs. Rowley and Caroline, "I don't know if it was a male or female mouse. So, if it's a male, I'm calling it Henry (that's not the actual name Mr. Rowley used, but I know for libel reasons I can't repeat the real one) after my obnoxious friend Henry. And if it's a female her name is Sally (that's not the actual name either, but for libel reasons, I've changed it, too)." Sally is the name of a woman who works in a club Mrs. Rowley belongs to and constantly makes mistakes, upsetting my mistress.

Anyway, Henry and Sally reappeared the other night. I was lying on the couch next to Mrs. Rowley and Caroline as they watched TV. They scampered across the floor in tandem, and the next thing I knew, Caroline had hurled a glass at them, which shattered. Then I saw Mr. Rowley appear in his pajamas, grumbling. Mrs. Rowley asked him to pick up the pieces, which he did, kneeling on the carpeted floor. I then heard him complain to Caroline, "I just cut my finger on a glass fragment."

I love the Rowleys. Photo by Matthew Schaeffer.

The next day, I discovered I couldn't go into the TV room because Mrs. Rowley had taped up the door. I heard that on the other side of the door, there were three mouse traps and a line of sticky papers with a bit of cheese in the middle of each one. For two whole days, I was banned from that room. But then I heard Mr. Rowley say he had crept into the TV room from another door and seen no dead mice.

The following morning, Mr. Rowley took me out at seven-thirty, and he ran into Mr. Peter Phillips, who is a lawyer and chairman of the board of my cooperative building. Mr. Phillips was stretching his long angular frame by one of the metal brass poles holding up the awning. I guess Mr. Phillips had gone running instead of bicycling, which I know he likes to do because I often see his bike parked on the side of the building near where I so often do my business, though I am careful not to emit a stream of my golden-colored urine near his tires.

I heard Mr. Phillips say to my boss, "How are the mice?"

"I've renamed them Henry and Sally, Henry after an obnoxious friend of mine, and Sally after a nitwit Terez knows. But we think they ate the poison and went back inside the walls to die."

Mr. Phillips said, "I can tell you what happened. The older mouse catches his whiskers on the sticky stuff and then retreats before getting caught. He then warns the baby mice. Be careful when you see Henry or Sally and call their names as the human Henry or Sally may come running instead!"

But the mystery to me is if they did not eat the cheese on the sticky paper and on the traps, are they still alive inside the walls of my apartment? I will have to wait and hear if Mr. Rowley asks for an explanation from Alec, our superintendent, inquiring whether the cheese on the paper and the traps was poisoned.

Mr. Rowley told me his hairdresser, Jamie, said I am the right kind of dog for a three-dog night. Apparently, a hunter would stave off the cold while overnighting in the woods, warmed by three big basset hounds such as myself.

The day before yesterday, Mrs. Rowley fell on her knees on the floor in front of me. She gave me a big hug. I could feel her pretty blond hair against my ears and her lips on my head. My lips started to move rapidly up and down. I was talking to her, telling dear Mrs. Rowley all my hopes and fears, mostly hopes and some dreams. "Mmmm … mmm," she says.

"Grummm," I growl softly and gently.

"Tell me all of your story," says Mrs. Rowley.

"Grummm," I tell her everything.

You know the meaning of ornery. I am sometimes ornery. Like this morning, for example. I had whacked my tail a few times while lying beside my dear Mrs. Rowley in the bedroom as the air conditioner made its endless loud sound, though sometimes it takes a rest and stops. Anyway nobody heard me, including Peter Rowley on the other side of the bed.

Then some while later, I padded out of my enclosed area. What often happens is that Mrs. Rowley sort of traps me in the small space between her two big closets lying on my little round bed, but she's not very careful about completely blocking my escape route. When I've had my eight hours sleep and enough of that air conditioner's noise, I emerge. And I'm also thirsty. Whack of tail. Nothing happens, but then Mr. Rowley rises halfway up in the bed, sees me, and gets up. He opens the bedroom door, and I go out. After, he says in his friendly but impatient way, "Go on," I head for the kitchen, his foot not touching my head but guiding me toward his office, which is a shorter way to the kitchen rather than around by the living room and dining room.

Then I drink from my metal water bowl. Mr. Rowley shuts the office door, and he blocks the other exit from the kitchen, which is into the dining room, with a portable fence. I wait. And I wait. Mr. Rowley has not supplied me with another round basset hound bed, which he does sometimes, but it's comfortable in the kitchen because the air conditioners have been on in the rest of the apartment, and the imitation stone tile floor is cool, and I like resting my big, long body (I've been putting on a little weight recently) on it. I wait some more.

Having dressed, Mr. Rowley comes back, makes coffee, and goes away to drink it. I know he likes to drink his coffee with hot milk sitting in his favorite hard chair with a soft yellow cushion on it in front of the window looking east over the Upper East Side toward Queens. Almost directly beneath him, a hundred feet down, is the roof of Temple Israel, where on one side is a wheelbarrow in the shape of a duck. I know this because one day he told me, because I'm too low down to be able to see anything.

Anyway, he comes back into the kitchen, takes my poo-poo plastic bags and my four tiny dog biscuits, puts them in his pocket, and picks up my old red leash. "Come on," he says holding open the rear door of the kitchen leading to the service elevator. "Come on," he repeats. But I don't move, even though I'm dying to go out. Finally he walks over, attaches the leash to my collar, and before he can pull me by the neck, I amble out of the kitchen and proceed toward the elevator.

I am feeling unwell in this heat. It's early morning. I have diarrhea. Mr. Rowley has already taken me out where I did Nos. 1 and 2, but part of the latter was very loose. I can't hold back any longer. But I love the Rowleys, and I like their oriental carpets. So I head into the new room where there are now lots of boxes and an ordinary carpet. Ah, relief! But the smell is strong, so I walk out to the living room, where there is less odor.

Yesterday, I heard Mrs. Rowley and the architect say that construction will start soon on the new little penthouse above my apartment (it's also the Rowleys').

I just now discovered how I apparently lost my opportunity for everlasting fame! I heard Letitia tell Mr. Rowley that Jon David (he's my body washer) phoned Letitia and had said *The View*, a television show, wanted a basset hound for Jon to wash. Millions of people would have watched me, but sadly, I was on vacation in Queens, and the Rowleys were on vacation in Italy, and Letitia did not know where to contact my owners for permission. What a pity. I might have met Barbara Walters. She might have given me a kiss!

Anyway, the Rowleys are now back from Europe, and Caroline just gave me a hug, making me squeal with pleasure while wagging my tail.

Mr. Rowley is a handsome man, even if he's in his seventy-fifth year, and this morning, he was wearing red trousers, a bright yellow sports shirt, and polished brown shoes. The ensemble set off his tanned face, arms, and neck, gained from the two-week stay in Italy which they did not take me along on, yours truly being banished to Queens. Anyway, this pretty young woman with a good figure, walking west on Seventy-Fifth Street, sees Mr. Rowley hanging onto me with my dirty red-dog rope attached to that painful collar around my neck. I was trying to drag him into the street as I did my No. 1. The attractive young thing smiled broadly, showing her white teeth. I didn't think it was funny, but I'm only a dog, and a basset hound at that. Basset hounds have a different sense of humor from other dogs, which is probably due to sensitivity over our ears, which people are always making fun of.

One of the things about myself which I don't mind is the smell I make when I do No. 1 while supposedly lying asleep just below Mrs. Rowley. It's all me. It's an acrid smell like old wood.

I have to ask myself: What is Boss Rowley carrying on about now? He stands up above me, holding two sheets of paper as I recline in my super new bed, one ear flopping over my eye, reading a speech. Then he comes to a sentence: "Dorothy McGuire loses her pacifism temporarily to save her pet goose from a Southern soldier's supper." But I'm not a goose. Apparently, he's introducing an excerpt from a film, *Friendly Persuasion,* at an arts club he belongs to. He looks at me. I guess I should be happy that another animal's life is saved.

TRUE LOVE

A most startling event! I had heard some talk about this over the past few weeks, but no one, including Mr. Rowley, my beloved Mrs. Rowley, Caroline Rowley, Letitia, or even or even that pretty young English girl Diana, my temporary basset sitter had said anything to yours directly. But I met a small, black cockerpoo this morning at someone else's apartment. This little black creature—much smaller than me—and I kissed! The cockerpoo had to lift his head to reach mine. I was in heaven! Eye to eye. Wet nose to nose.

That little black dog and I had fallen in love. Then he was promptly given away to someone else!

Perhaps to help make up for my loss, Mrs. Rowley has given me a super basset bed. It just goes to show if you treat humans okay, they'll treat you okay. It's shaped like a half moon with a big soft bluey-white mattress, a back like a half moon, and an opening on the other half. It must be the Tiffany of dog beds. *So* I've given up my habit of doing No.1 on the floor around my bed on the white carpets Mrs. Rowley energetically drapes on the floor.

But a sudden and most blissful reversal of fortune! My companion returned—my pet, my significant other, or whatever. It turns out my cockerpoo was not given away! Luckily, the prospective new owner changed his or her silly human mind.

The poodle's name is … I can't remember now. Will miracles never cease? She's not entirely respectful, although in fact she's a he. It's very rare that a basset admits to making a mistake. My mistake.

He jumps on my rear and humps away until I get tired of the irritation, and with a powerful turn of my hips, I force him off. He weighs only six pounds. I heard Mr. Rowley quote Graham Greene (whoever he is) in *A Burnt-Out Case*, describing a couple having sex in the jungle in Africa. The narrator observed the man and woman were lepers and surmised that God was not entirely serious when he invented the sex act.

Getting back to my new friend, the cockerpoo. It's all too staggering for words. My sixty-five pounds frighten him. When he steps on my paws or tries to grab my cookie, I growl.

But I love him. I love him! All six pounds of him, running around, curving, scrambling, bouncing, and racing. I only wish I could go as fast. And she squeaks, really squeaks! I mean *he.*

I'm gladder than ever that I left the O'Dell farm in South Jersey.

The Rowleys want to give this little black thing a name. When my new friend was sent off during the day to be trained by Pat McGregor, the trainer, Pat said he had to have a name. There were a number of possibilities, including Frank, Jim, Blackie, Thing, Henry, Boniface, Poodle, Dog, Mutt, Pete, Maxwell, George, Fido, Engelbert, Laszlo, Miklos, or Chauncey. Fortunately, they chose none of them. I don't remember who, but someone said Bo Jackson. And there was also Bo Diddley. I heard Bo Jackson was an athlete or jazz musician some years ago.

In any case, everybody liked the name of Bo. But then there was disagreement between the Rowleys and Letitia over the spelling. The Rowleys liked Bo, but Letitia preferred Beau. Her voice rising, she said, "He's so beautiful." I like Bo better. Bo is shorter.

Bo likes to talk.

Of course, the Rowleys expected Bo would not make messes, but he immediately did—everywhere. Sounds familiar, doesn't it? I'm now reformed. As if I didn't know, the Rowleys say I'm a good dog. Because Bo eats so much he leaves many such horrors. Mr. and Mrs. Rowley already stepped in Bo's No. 2.

The Rowleys bought a gate and fitted it into the kitchen door that leads to the dining room. Bo squeezed through the bars. This was an accomplishment, because Bo's head and body are only fractionally smaller than the space between the bars.

Then Mrs. Rowley put a board against the bars. Bo pushed it over. Then Mrs. Rowley placed a chair against the board, but Bo, using all of his six pounds, forced the board and the chair back. Again he escaped. Then Mrs. Rowley put a basket full of books on the chair. This seemed to stop him.

Bo began to shriek. I said to myself, "How can such a small dog make so much noise?"

Today, Bo actually used the blue bathroom pad he's supposed to. He's starting to be trained.

I barked or spoke too soon (I can do both). Bo emerged from Caroline's room and struck again. An angry Mr. Rowley said, "I had to restrain myself from not tossing Bo out of a window above the synagogue. It's a ten-story fall. I would never have to do it again."

Bo was again locked up in the kitchen, and Mr. Rowley cleverly designed a new barrier using the marble board, the existing gate, two of the old portable gates, a big chair from the dining room, and two high chairs from the kitchen table. Mr. Rowley took me outside where I did my duty for God, country, and New York, including Mayor Bloomberg, the city council, and the sanitation department! Bo was effectively trapped.

Last night, during the early stages of the election results, Mrs. Rowley was tired from negotiating with the contractor over the new penthouse where Caroline will live with Bo. Mrs. Rowley left the kitchen door open. I heard Mr. Rowley let out a shout. What had happened? Bo had run from the kitchen, through the apartment into their bedroom, and had stood on his hind legs. Caroline offered this morning, "If he had eaten chocolates, he could've been poisoned—chocolate is poisonous to dogs." He had indeed been starting to eat the boss's chocolates.

This morning, it's gray and drizzly. Mr. Rowley equips himself as usual with a small umbrella, but doesn't give me one or even share his with me. Coming up the street near Temple Israel, I see the brown and white beagle. Rowley had me on a looser leash than normal. The beagle starts to yelp, lunging toward me, held back by only his leash. Both his owners were walking him, the wife holding the leash. I jump toward the beagle, barking and coming within inches of biting him or her, which would teach him or her a lesson. The couple and Mr. Rowley grin, and I feel exhilarated!

I walk into 815's lobby, and there is Jay. Wagging my tail from the memory of my triumph over the beagle and glad to see Jay, I do some basset jumps and start to bark until finally Mr. Rowley says, "That's enough." I walk happily to the service elevator, pulling Mr. Rowley behind me.

There is a strange, somewhat suspicious man in an adjoining building who parks his bike, locking it to a lamppost opposite the side entrance of 815 Park. With Mr. Rowley's encouragement, I urinate on the sloping sidewalk, hoping my yellow urine will reach the bike, but it is trapped in the space between the pavement slabs. Better luck next time.

Then I go inside. Earlier in the day, I had heard Caroline say, "I put Bo in the kitchen during the night because he kept nibbling my face." Mr. Rowley replied, "Perhaps he was hungry."

When I came in, Mr. Rowley said, "Look! There's Bo's dinner from last night. We forgot to feed him." It was still on top of the counter. I soon saw Bo happily eating. In fact, after a while, he started trying to eat the yellow plastic top to the eating bowl, chasing it around the kitchen floor.

The Rowleys were really irritated at Bo last night. "What are we going to do with him?" said Mrs. Rowley.

Mr. Rowley said, "We could eat him. Poodle au vin."

I was still sleeping quietly in my blue round bed at nine-fifteen Friday morning when Mr. Rowley came in to the living room and said, referring to me, "The world's laziest dog." I noticed he was wearing a tennis warm-up suit and sneakers. He must have just lost his early morning tennis match.

Mr. Rowley thinks I can't tell one doorman from another, because he clearly has a biased attitude against all nonspeaking animals such as myself. This is because I surprised him by suddenly tugging on my leash outside our building and scrambling over to

Mohammed for a quick caress and pat. Mr. Rowley thinks I have a special place in my basset heart only for Jay, but I am also very fond of Mohammed, who is from Yemen. He has nine children back in his home country. I know he used to work at 815 Park twenty or so years ago, and they gave him a going-away party. He already had three children at that point, and while he was away, he had six more. Now he is back here, looking a bit older, with a part-time job as a substitute doorman and handyman. So it goes!

Thank God! As much as I love little Bo, he is mercifully spending the weekend with Letitia. Which means peace! No little animal smelling my private parts, nor is he trying to sexually assault me. I was very sorry to overhear Mr. Rowley proudly telling Letitia that he had talked Mrs. Rowley out of having Bo castrated.

It's snowy outside. I pad into the lobby and see Mr. X with another elderly stocky man. I know Mr. X has accepted a lot of hospitality from the Rowleys but has never really reciprocated. As I get closer to him, even though I am on a leash, I leap at Mr. X's ankle, snarling. Mr. Rowley says without conviction, feigning shock and disapproval, "Amelia." I love the Rowleys, and their enemies are mine. I am glad I live with the Rowleys on Park and not with the O'Dells in Gibbsboro.

In the middle of the night, sleeping on the floor next to Mrs. Rowley in my super-basset-sized bed, I let out a loud groan. I must have been having a dream, perhaps about male bassets making love to me. I know this is not the first time I've done this. I always wake up Mr. or Mrs. Rowley—it's kind of a wild primitive sound. I'm pretty good at it--perhaps my ancestors up in heaven hear me. I hope so. Life for a basset hound--even on Park Avenue--is not easy: maybe they, i.e. my forebears, will come down and rescue me. I could have been dreaming about the O'Dells and Gibbsboro.

Mr. Rowley's not too smart! I was in his office, and I wanted the door to the kitchen to be opened so that I could get a drink. He was sitting at his computer. I had to pad up beside him and make grunting noises, slathering a bit of saliva on his knee. Then he got up and opened the door!

Valentine's Day! I happen to love Jay's brown leather shoes. I wag my tail and swivel my body. Jay grunts and squeals, "Amelia," in his guttural Hispanic voice. I lick his shoes. Lest I overlooked this detail earlier, Jay is from the country of Colombia.

Last night, Ramazan and Gente claimed I was limping. I wasn't limping, but when I sleep all afternoon and evening, my front left leg goes to sleep.

This morning, the boss repeated Ramazan and Gente's observation to dear Letitia, who said, "I'll consult Avra, my vet. My dogs get … [she cited some drug I've never heard of] for their arthritis. Her eyebrows [meaning mine] are turning gray." I'll have to look in a mirror.

The boss said, "Okay."

I wagged my tail after the boss said, "You know we're talking about you, Amelia."

Letitia continued cleaning my ears.

You may have wondered how I write my tale, and I don't mean wag it, being a dog and all that. Sometimes, I put a ballpoint (biro in English English) between my front left paw's two front left toes. Other times, I dictate it into my tape recorder, but since I don't talk, I have concealed this accomplishment from everyone but you, dear reader.

And, of course, in this modern era, I write most of it on my laptop, which, when Mr. Rowley is not looking, I transfer by a complicated process onto his computer. Of course, you may not believe the above. So I can only just say that using ESP, I transmit my story to Mr. Rowley, who records it for posterity in the annals of basset history.

How I'm writing my memoir is the truth, nothing but the truth, so help me, God. Oh God of all basset hounds and people. I put my paw on the Bible. I swear it!

That idiot, Mr. Rowley, is also trying to write a book about me, and to top it all off, he thinks he's a photographer. Yesterday afternoon, I had to wait before re-entering my building until Mr. Rowley came down from the fifteenth floor. Pretending we were returning home, Letitia first dragged me away from the building and then allowed me to pad toward it. All this time, Mr. Rowley was clicking away with his old-fashioned Nikon until he fell into the flowerbed beside the entrance, landing on the spikes of the retaining sides. He was helped to his feet by a couple of pretty young women, which Mr. Rowley did not seem unhappy about. I hope the photos come out, but I have my doubts. It was lucky he was wearing his black winter coat. It's cashmere. Why hasn't he bought me one?

It suddenly occurs to me that the reason I am a subdued basset hound is because of the way I was treated by the O'Dells in Gibbsboro. The late Flora had a happy childhood, waddling around on the concrete floor of the basset nursery surrounded by other happy little bassets. Flora, as you know, would leap onto any surface to get food. If I did that as a puppy, the O'Dells would have hit me. So I stay on the ground and look up enviously at pasta, lamb chops, potatoes, vegetables, and hot dogs.

Mr. Rowley has given me the name of Monster Mutt. I hope he's joking. You must remember that I had a very unhappy childhood. I can't help it if I sometimes snarl at dogs the same size or bigger than me. I know I've been known to snap at them. At other times, my disposition is what you might call undemonstrative. But those who love me without reservation, I love in return.

News flash: Tommy Hilfiger's ex-wife has moved in next door to me with her son and her brother. I hear she pays $50,000 a month for her triplex apartment, which ain't dog food.

This morning at six, Daddy Rowley tried to hook my leash to my collar and then fell to the ground beside me with a cramp. Mrs. Rowley, who was snugly sleeping above me, said sweetly, "I'll take her into the kitchen at seven." Dear Mrs. Rowley.

Later in the morning, I overheard Mr. Rowley telling Mrs. Rowley, "There was a big crowd of press people with TV cameras outside of Lenox Hill Hospital early this morning. They were there because Natasha Richardson was in the hospital after her ski accident. She's the wife of Liam Neeson, and her mother is Vanessa Redgrave." I often walk past the Seventy-Sixth Street corner of the hospital, though the journalists were by the main entrance of the hospital on Seventy-Seventh Street.

I hope basset hounds will be given a vote at the United Nations. Photo by Matthew Schaeffer.

The other morning, one of the doormen said to Rowley and me, "Three Merrill Lynch executives who got enormous bonuses have their pictures on the front of today's *Wall Street Journal*. One of them [he mentioned his name] lives in the big apartment building on the same side of the avenue thirty feet south of us. We see this guy walking two bulldogs every day." Why can't I get big money like that?!

Mr. Rowley says, "Come on, crazy dog."

I lift an eyebrow.

Two nights later, I'm out on my walk pulling Mr. Rowley along, and I suddenly see this youngish guy come out of 799 Park pulling two small dogs. I'm guessing that's the Merrill Lynch guy. He acts very confident, but paradoxically a little bit frightened too. He's got short well-groomed hair, a stylish open-neck sports shirt, and a trim body.

With determined strides, he walks the two little dogs rapidly. He obviously gets what he wants, and he looks like one of those handsome, hard-driving young executives. No wonder he got $10 million before Merrill Lynch nearly went bankrupt and was sold to Bank of America.

Spring is here, and the flowers are blooming in the window planters along my route. I'm walking with Letitia up Seventy-Fifth Street toward Madison Avenue when I see this beautiful big white dog. I have no idea what breed it is, but I instantly fall in love. Now, I don't usually like dogs that are bigger than me, but this one has something special. So instead of going up my favorite side of the street, I pull Letitia across the street and follow my heartthrob until we get close to them. Then Letitia says to the man holding the white dog, "My basset's in love with your dog." He smiles. It's true. I am in love.

That young woman vet came to my apartment yesterday and stuck a needle in a small white growth on my forehead just above my right eye. What was that about? I hope it was nothing serious—there was just a small red mark where the needle went in and of course came out. I saw Mr. Rowley looking at my forehead again when he and I went out this morning. About an hour later, I let out a grunt, which I like to do sometimes, and there was another grunt from some distance away. I realized it was Rowley imitating me.

Letitia arrives.

Rowley says, "What do you think of Amelia's cyst?"

Letitia looks at my bump. "It's gone down a little. If I put a hot compress on it, it will go down a little faster. Do you have a waterproof plastic bag?"

Mr. Rowley goes to see Mrs. Rowley, returns and looks deep into a drawer near the GE refrigerator, and then hands a bag to Letitia.

"Is it waterproof?" says Letitia.

Rowley replies, "If you seal it properly, it will be."

Letitia takes me out.

The night before last, Mr. Rowley dreamt I was at the top of a snow-covered hill starting to slide successfully down on my haunches toward him. Then he woke up and left the apartment at quarter to six in the morning to go to Newark airport to take a flight to England. I shall miss Caroline and her father, but fortunately, Mrs. Rowley is staying here, and she will probably let me sleep in the big bed with her.

The next day, Mrs. Rowley went to a health farm called Canyon Ranch for a much-needed rest from the builders who are building Caroline's penthouse and connecting it by a spiral staircase to my apartment. Bo, my dear fluffy friend and Caroline's dog, will live upstairs. Not all was lost, however, as I spent four very fun nights with Jay, his wife, his mother, and his daughter.

Upon his return from the old country, Mr. Rowley told me that there is a cock pheasant in the garden of the Rowley house in the county of Rutland called Attila who lives there all during the hunting season, from October to March. Attila has beautiful gold and red feathers and a black beak. In the spring, Attila makes a lot of noise flapping his wings, hoping a female will fly in to join him. Sometimes, one or two ladies fly over the wall. Of course, later in the spring and summer, Attila flies out to the fields.

Mr. Rowley told me there is also a big black crow who regards as his territory the roof above Mr. Rowley's office on the top floor of his house. So whenever Rowley first arrives after his flight from New York, the crow gets very annoyed and bangs with his beak against a glass skylight, always frightening Rowley the first few times.

Rowley told me just before he left England yesterday to return to New York that he was standing at the window in the small sitting room of his manor house, which the Rowleys' part-time cook, Melony, calls the snug. He had just finished breakfast and was gazing at the green lawn and the box hedge that runs along one side of the gravel drive. A female pheasant with gray feathers speckled with white suddenly appeared in the near distance, walking purposefully along the hedge, and then abruptly turned left at the far end. Rowley knows this is where Attila goes in. Attila was no doubt waiting there for his lover.

I was astonished to hear that our new president, Barack Obama, has chosen a dog with the same name as my friend Bo for his daughters and wife, Michelle. He's a Portuguese something and was a gift from Senator Ted Kennedy, whoever he is.

A final indignity! Mr. Rowley, who thinks he's writing this book, transcribing my thoughts onto his laptop, had the nerve to drag me to Central Park early this morning just so he could photograph me and Bo. I do not like to move quickly—or at least I like to amble along at my pace, not Rowley's. So I stalled him many times before we reached Seventy-Sixth and Fifth. Twice, I brought him to a jolting halt, and I thought he would fall over, but he didn't.

We could see Letitia in the distance surrounded by several small dogs, including my friend Bo. She waved to us, and we went for a long walk among the daffodils and flowering white trees, up and down steps. It was quite exhausting, but I chased Bo, and he chased me, and I sniffed a number of other dogs. Rowley rewarded me in the service elevator back to my apartment with three yummy dog cookies. Of course, he had taken a lot of photos of me, and I hope they turned out well. Mr. Rowley was using an old-fashioned Nikon with color slide film when I know modern photographers prefer digital, but I still love old Rowley, and I'm sure he'll tell the truth about me.

It's a beautiful spring morning. Mrs. Rowley brings me into the kitchen where Mr. Rowley is, and I'm hoping he's going to take me out. But instead he gets the portable gate, preventing me from escaping into the living room, which is more comfortable than the hard kitchen floor. There's not even a loose white carpet on the floor for me to lie my long body and ears on. What's going on? I stand on my paws on the hard floor. Mr. Rowley disappears, making sure before he goes that the gate stays in place. But after a short while, he comes back with my smaller blue-gray bed and drops it for me near the kitchen door. At least I can lie in comfort, but he still doesn't take me out, which is really very inconsiderate. After all basset hounds have to go to the bathroom like everyone else, and it was twelve hours ago when I last hit the street! Mr. Rowley makes his breakfast, maneuvers around my gate, and carries his tray away with all sorts of delicious food on it, none of which is offered to me.

I was only slightly less amused when Mr. Rowley later told me of a conversation he had had at lunch at the Union Club. Basset hounds are not allowed in the dining room, which is why I wasn't there. In fact, Mrs. Rowley is not allowed to be a member, being a female, although as a human, she could have been present at the lunch. Rowley was discussing with his friend, Warren Adler, the author of *The War of the Roses*, and his new friend, Stephen Greenwald, an old friend of Warren's and a film executive, the possibility of making a movie about Mrs. Rowley's attempted escapes from Hungary many years before.

Mr. Rowley mentioned he was helping me write my memoir when Warren suddenly said, "That's the dog that made a mess in the living room of their country house when Sunny and I were the Rowleys' guests one summer weekend. If it was my dog, I'd have beaten the shit out of it!"

Mr. Rowley said, "We weren't bad hosts. Terez and I don't believe in hitting our dog."

I should think not!

Why is it that some people think of basset hounds only in terms of our bathroom habits? This morning, Sid Shapiro, the clock repairman arrived in our vestibule. I greeted him in a friendly way, not biting him and wagging my tail. Mr. Shapiro, who is quite old, maneuvered around my large body, pulling his clock repair kit on wheels. I heard Mr. Rowley and Mr. Shapiro reminisce that it had been twenty-four years since Mr. Shapiro had been in our apartment.

"Do you remember," Mr. Rowley said, "that when you were here before, Amelia's predecessor had left a mess on the carpet and you stepped in it?"

Mr. Shapiro said he didn't recall the incident.

There was also a discussion between Rowley and Shapiro over my sex and name. "Amelia's a she."

"I thought you said 'Emilio,'" replied Mr. Shapiro. Won't they ever learn?

It was drizzling unpleasantly when Mr. Rowley introduced me, "Tom, this is Amelia. Amelia, Mr. Trowbridge."

Tom Trowbridge is a lawyer who writes golf books.

"I'm writing a book about our basset hound, *Memoir of a Park Avenue Basset Hound*."

How dare Boss Rowley lie! I'm writing the book!

"I can only hope I'm in the book," said Trowbridge.

"I can't remember."

In fact, my memory is better than my owner's. This is Tom's first appearance in my memoir.

I am pulling Rowley on my leash past Puffy's old building, now completely renovated with three new tenants. The building has just been occupied.

Coming out of the gold-colored metal front doors is a handsome young black man with a wide smile. "Do you know how to tie a tie?" he asks Mr. Rowley.

I suddenly sense Mr. Rowley becoming tense.

Then Rowley replies, "Sure. Can you please hold my dog?"

The doorman hands my boss a yellow tie. Rowley ties it around his own neck, loosens it, lifts it over his head and gives the cravat back to the doorman, who slides it over his own head. Then he tightens the tie.

"Thanks, man. I'm Davey Robinson."

Davey hands my leash back to Boss Rowley.

"I'm Peter Rowley."

Needless to say, basset hounds (and most certainly lady bassets) never wear ties.

ESCAPE FROM DEATH

Somewhat to my surprise, I started behaving rather strangely last Tuesday morning. Because of delays on the subway, Boss Rowley was late in taking me out. I had already been holding back my poo-poo and pee-pee for twelve hours. It was another half hour before he took me down the elevator to the street. After fifteen minutes, I still had not done Nos. 1 and 2. I attributed this to the lazy misty morning of that late spring.

That evening, I was slow to go outside, but I did my duty. The next morning, it was more of the same. Rowley's friend Tim deWerff, a musician, crossing Park, said hello to him.

Rowley replied, "I've got a sick dog."

Later that morning, Letitia said she could not move me. Mr. Rowley said, "You have to be firm."

Letitia said, "She'll listen to you."

The boss demonstrated how with a little force I could be urged to leave the kitchen for the service elevator. Letitia took my leash, and I did not see him for half an hour, but we did go outside for a few gentle steps.

That night, I was almost impossible to move. Rowley finally dragged me into the elevator, but before he had gotten me in fully, one of my legs slipped into the space between the elevator and the wall of the shaft.

He said, "Shit." Rowley was alarmed. He carefully pulled my leg up and then the elevator went down. On the ground floor, my leg again slid into the space, and once more, he rescued it. He tried to pull me down the hall toward the front door, but I stayed on my haunches.

Mohammed said, "You'll have to get a cart for her." We returned to our apartment very slowly. Rowley and I knew the situation was serious.

That night, Terez and Peter carried my sixty-six pounds back to our bedroom and put me on the big round dog bed. As they lowered me, Peter fell on me, but neither of us were hurt.

The next morning, I still couldn't stand up. I was very thirsty. Boss Rowley brought a little saucer of water, and I drank it all, licking the bowl for every last drop. After Mrs. Rowley phoned her, Avra the vet arrived. She examined me. Avra, who probably weighs about 115 pounds, lifted me with Mrs. Rowley's help. I promptly pissed a long stream of dark yellow urine onto the white carpet, but it was not intentional. I couldn't help it.

I was returned to our kitchen. Avra said, "She's got to lose ten pounds. I'll give her a pain-killing shot …" She told the Rowleys to feed me a new kind of food and prescribed some pills. My head was shaking a little bit from nerves.

That afternoon, Mrs. Rowley and Avra took me to the New York City animal center on West Fifty-Fifth Street between Ninth and Tenth Avenues. I was frightened. I heard them say they were probably going to operate on me the next day after x-raying my body. I didn't know exactly what that meant. The hospital has a fresh new look about it, and the staff was mainly young. Everyone was friendly, and I found myself in a cage. I could hear other dogs in cages nearby. Most of them were quiet, but there was one who was crying, and another one barked. It was a big black dog.

The morning came, and I was not given anything to eat or drink. At least the Rowleys gave me some water. Then a man in a white coat, wearing a funny-looking device like a small tube hanging on a cord, came into my cell.

At that moment, Mrs. Rowley appeared. The man said to my mistress, "I'm Dr. Seaman. I'm going to operate on Amelia. We found a big disc that's causing the trouble. I'll be removing it."

What was going on?

The vet lifted me onto a table. He produced a needle, which I was afraid of, and inserted it into my right front leg. Mrs. Rowley was watching. Giving me a hug, she smiled at me, and I don't remember anything after that. The next morning I woke up with what I can only describe as a hangover, even though I've never had one. I could feel something funny in the middle of my back. Mrs. Rowley wasn't there—only the other dogs including the black one who still barked. I could see through the bars of my cage a translucent plastic wall and door. Nurses were moving about.

It was Saturday. About two hours later, Letitia turned up, saying in her Filipino accent, "Amelia. Poor Amelia." I was beginning to feel some pain in my back. I barked a few times, and Letitia said, "Sssh. Sssh." No sign of the Rowleys.

The next day, Letitia turned up again. But she didn't bring any dog biscuits. Crying, I told her I wanted to get out of there as fast as possible. I then tried barks and whines. Although she held me, she didn't take me through the door to freedom. Letitia said, "The Rowleys are away for the weekend." Couldn't they have picked another weekend to go away? Such behavior is un-American.

However, I tried to stand up, and to my great shock and annoyance, I found I could only raise myself with my front paws.

I had heard from other dogs that human beings sometimes kill us when we get old. Was this to be my fate? But surely they wouldn't have operated if they were planning to euthanize me, but you never know. And supposing the operation wasn't a success?

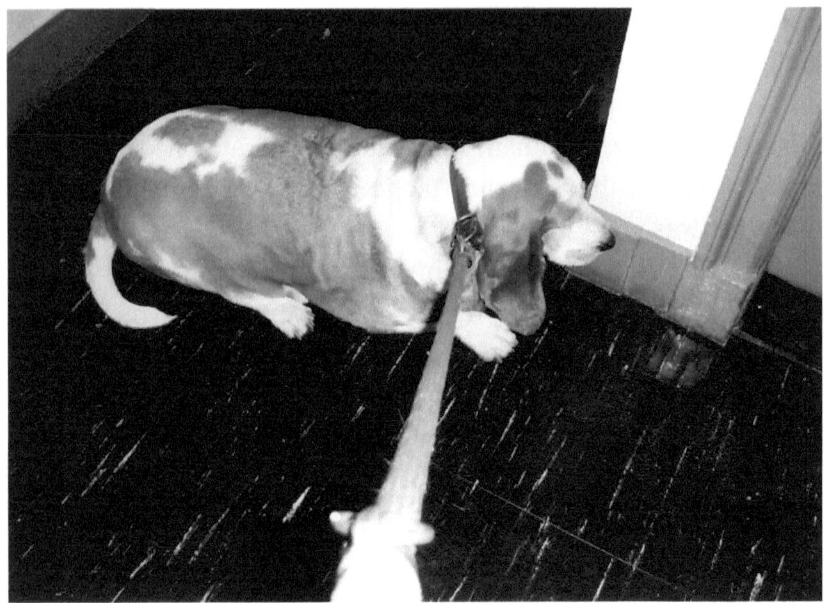

My ever-present leash.

The next day was Monday. I saw Peter and Terez Rowley through the glass door. Then they came in to the locked section where the sick dogs like me live. I wagged my tail energetically and started to crawl out of my cage. I was crying with excitement! Mrs. Rowley sank to the floor, started to cry and hugged me. This went on for quite a while, and Mr. Rowley stroked my head. There were tears in his eyes. A nurse loaned him a swivel chair. Mrs. Rowley asked Mr. Rowley, "Can I borrow your handkerchief?" He gave her his big yellow one with the white polka dots.

I suddenly thought I saw my chance and propelled myself as fast as I could toward the door and glass panel, but I couldn't escape. Then I ambled about in a circle around a group of cages. When the Rowleys left, I was very sad.

Over the next few days, I was visited by the Rowleys, Caroline, and Letitia. On Peter Rowley's third visit, I came out of my cell and let loose a big stream of urine. He stepped around it, and a nurse mopped it up. I heard a nurse say, "She's about the same. She's a little better. Her front legs are very strong." While Mr. Rowley sat on a chair above me, I rested my chin and my paws on the floor near his feet. Then the nurse put a sling under me and I was able to use my stronger right leg to help me get back into my cell. I watched the boss depart, and from outside the locked area, he waved to me.

Nobody visited me over the weekend. On Monday morning, Letitia came to see me. She told me that my boyfriend, Bo, had spent the night with the Rowleys and that he had done his duty outside in the street. Caroline was away in Locust Valley and the Hamptons playing golf. I hope she did well in the tournament. She was playing with a friend. I'm a pretty good golfer for a basset hound!

I heard Mrs. Rowley was not at all pleased with Bo's jumping up and scratching her legs, but she admitted no one had cut his nails. The Rowleys admired Bo's energy. Before Letitia left, I was helped with a sling back into my cage. I could tell from the expression on her pretty face that she thought my progress was only a slight improvement.

Amazing! Last night, as I was about to go to sleep after a well-earned day of doing nothing, Mrs. Rowley appeared, carrying my round blue bed. Was I glad to see her! She hugged and kissed me, and I squealed. Then she left the bed after saying to me, "You're going to a nursing home in Paramus. There's a ninety percent chance you'll learn to walk again [actually, I was quite enjoying this life of leisure]. I brought your bed so you'll have something familiar." I thought she was going to say goodbye in Hungarian, but she didn't. Then she left. So it goes!

Paramus. Where's Paramus?

Then Letitia turned up this morning. And lo and behold, Brother Rowley appeared this afternoon like the businessman/writer he is holding a black briefcase. For some mysterious reason, my cage had been moved three places down, and I could no longer see the nurses' station. Rowley asked for a chair, and I was hoisted out of my cage and put on a blanket beside him. He stroked my ears, chin, head, and back. Becoming bored with this, I started to explore a new way to escape. This time I shoved myself, along with my front paws and left leg, went a few feet down the aisle between the cages, turned left, and found myself facing the glass wall. I could see the nurses.

After swiveling left again, I continued to the glass door, but the staff prevented me from escaping. I let out a stream of yellow urine, and even when a middle-aged nurse with a bucket and mop came in to clean it up, I still couldn't get out. In fact, even Boss Rowley tricked me into moving a few feet away. After twenty or so minutes, my master asked one of the nurses to help me back into my cage. I settled on my bed, the very same that Mrs. Rowley had brought last night, and Boss Rowley waved his fingers, saying goodbye.

It's eight-thirty the next morning. My God! I was just enjoying a little more sleep after a peaceful night disturbed only by my neighbor's occasional bark. The nurses arrive with a stretcher followed by Mrs. Rowley. I knew something was cooking.

"We're off to Paramus," my mistress said. I still don't know where Paramus is.

"In New Jersey," I heard my mistress respond.

Oh, no! Back to New Jersey and the O'Dells. What have I done to deserve such a fate? It's not my fault my hind legs gave out. All those extra cookies and fattening food. Ten pounds overweight! At least I was starting to lose a few pounds here at the west side medical center. Back at the O'Dells, I would balloon again! But on second thought, Paramus doesn't sound like Gibbsboro, where I was born. Maybe there's hope.

The nurses put me on a stretcher.

I lay on the stretcher on two back seats of Caesar's white SUV, Mrs. Rowley sitting on the floor beside me near my head. Another seat had been removed. Caesar is a Peruvian who sometimes drives the Rowleys. I looked appealingly at the nurses who had carried me, but they just smiled and waved.

To my surprise, Paramus is near the Hudson River. They carried me into a nursing home. The vet said, "She'll get an hour's therapy five days a week until August 6."

My new residence was clean and cheerful. I was grateful it was not the O'Dell basset hound farm.

I wonder what the Rowleys are doing in my absence. Are they sorry I am not there? Do they miss my occasional decorating of their carpets? Where is Bo? Is he with Letitia, or have the Rowleys brought him in as a replacement for me—temporarily, that is? As soon as I recover, I shall return, as General MacArthur said, and join Bo in the Rowleys' duplex. Having Bo as a companion will take away my loneliness when the Rowleys are out of the apartment. I don't imagine I will be able to climb the spiral staircase to Caroline's penthouse, but perhaps Bo will be able to scamper down it to see me. And when Caroline is at work in her art gallery, I am sure Bo will yap so much that the senior Rowleys will bring him downstairs. He may even start writing a memoir of his own, *The Adventures of Bo.*

Whoopee! I overheard my new doctor (I never can remember his name) say on the phone to Terez Rowley's answering machine, "Amelia is doing very well. She is using both legs when we carry her in a sling. By July 20, she should be walking a bit." July 20 is Peter Rowley's birthday. This will be my gift to him.

My ESP told me that the Rowleys might be visiting very soon at my new residence at the Oradell Animal Hospital in Paramus.

I guessed that Peter Rowley would start making jokes to Mrs. Rowley about Paramus, New Jersey, like "Paramus is famous for its food." Anyway, Mr. and Mrs. Rowley did indeed turn up today at about 1 p.m. I was helped into the waiting room by a rather plump nurse named Samantha, whom I like. Despite wearing a red form-fitting wool dress, Mrs. Rowley got down on the floor and welcomed me with hugs, kisses, and her usual tears. No tears from Mr. Rowley this time. He sat on a chair above us and stroked my back, head, chin, and soft, floppy ears. Mr. Rowley gave Mrs. Rowley his handkerchief.

Peter Rowley said, "She's lost a pound or two."

My mistress replied, "You think so?"

"And her hair has mostly grown back."

After a while, I propelled myself with my front legs around the floor and actually stood up for a moment. Both the Rowleys seemed very pleased, marveling at my feat. Then I lay on the floor, and Mr. and Mrs. Rowley continued to caress me. I placed my head between Mr. Rowley's shoes, and Mrs. Rowley gave me two carrots. I let out a series of contented grunts, sort of halfway between a purr and a growl. I was very happy.

Eventually, I noticed the boss press a button on the wall behind him. It started to flash. I sensed the Rowleys were signaling to the staff they were about to go. No one appeared. Mrs. Rowley said, "You'll have to open that door and ask for someone." Two young nurses helped me out of the waiting room using a sling and a leash. I could see out of the corner of my eye the Rowleys wave goodbye.

Now I'm still wondering if Bo has been staying with the Rowleys. Has he replaced me in their affections? Is he trained? But of course, I will soon be back, as soon as I can walk again. My ESP tells me Bo was a good dog when he stayed with the Rowleys over this Fourth of July weekend.

I also sensed that Bo was in their Toyota Sienna in high-speed traffic when a muffler, lying in the New York Thruway, ricocheted from a car in front and struck their windshield, forcing them to pull off the highway. They were going 70 mph, and the gas muffler must have been going another seventy. The outer glass shattered, but the plastic holding the inner and outer glass held firm, although Mr. Rowley was covered with a coat of fine glass. Mr. Rowley had raised his left arm to protect his eyes and face.

The state police came. The state trooper, Officer de Silva, said, "You're not allowed to drive this van any more." Rowley and the officer studied the windshield. Rowley said, "There's brown paint on the broken windshield."

De Silva said, "I'll go and look for the muffler along the roadside afterward." Then a tow truck arrived. The driver loaned Rowley a glove to brush the glass off his arms and sports shirt. Rowley sat in the front seat of the truck. The tow truck operator winched the van onto the body of the truck. Mrs. Rowley, Bo, and their three guests stayed in the van. Bo later returned to New York in a Lincoln Towncar, which the Rowleys had to rent from Avis at Newburgh airport. Bo got to sit on Mrs. Rowley's lap.

The happy day has come! This morning, I heard the nurses say I would be going home. I was so excited that I could barely restrain myself in my basset hound body. When would they come? And would it be Mrs. Rowley, Caroline, Peter, Letitia, or all of them together?

I was very popular here. The nurses said, "Amelia's such a sweet, gentle dog. We all love her."

That afternoon, I was walking into a waiting room. I can walk now—with no sling. And I weigh ten pounds less. I am a svelte basset hound, if there is such a thing—only fifty-five pounds.

There was my dear mistress with a big smile, holding out her arms. I ran toward her. I thought she would cry, but she didn't. She exclaimed, "Amelia. Amelia, darling!" She hugged me and led me to the white SUV outside. Soon, I was on Route 4 and then going over the George Washington Bridge into New York. And then I was at my building. Before I knew it, I was getting off the elevator and running into our apartment. I let out several barks, and I ran into the bedroom, where I saw Peter Rowley. More barks. He stroked my back, and I swiveled around squealing. And Peter Rowley was taking pictures. I happily settled into my big round bed in the living room. And then Letitia came, and she gave me some dog food. Was I ever happy!

The Rowleys and Letitia are always pulling me around by my neck. I hate that collar and the leash. That's one of the reasons I'm so stubborn! Yesterday, Letitia took a harness the hospital had given the Rowleys. She put my front paws through it and fastened it between my shoulders on my back. Then she taught Mr. and Mrs. Rowley how to do it. I must admit that I rather like walking around outside doing my business, wearing this red harness!

Bo arrived today. He was staying with Letitia while I was convalescing. Bo and I started playing. I tried to steal his food. He has these little brown pellets. I am always hungry since the hospital, the Rowleys and Letitia made me lose ten pounds for health reasons. However, Letitia snatched away Bo's pellets before I could eat too many of them.

In the service elevator this morning, as Bo and I and Boss Rowley were on our way down to the sidewalks of 815 Park Avenue, Bo licked my face, cleaning it for me. I now think of Bo as my son, because, as you know, dear reader, I was fixed early in my life by the Rowleys to prevent me from having little Amelias or Floras or Bos.

Once outside, the boss struggled to control both Bo and me on our leashes. Jay, the doorman I love, was watering down the sidewalk while a group of children and parents prepared to board a school bus on the corner of Park and Seventy-Fifth. I dropped a nice little No. 2 deposit right in front of the bus door.

Jay exclaimed, "Look at that!" He was annoyed.

Mr. Rowley said guiltily, "Was it Amelia?"

"Yes," replied Jay who could not be too sharp with the boss as he is only a doorman and Mrs. Rowley is on the board of 815 Park.

Mr. Rowley dragged me and Bo back to the scene of my crime. He leaned over and picked up my poo-poo in his little black plastic bag and tossed it into the garbage can on the corner. However, since it was crumbly, he had to go back and pick up the remnants in a second bag.

Jay said, "That's okay."

Bo then did his business down by the synagogue. The boss picked that up in a third plastic bag. He then pulled Bo and me back along the sidewalk. Jay continued watering down the sidewalk on Seventy-Fifth Street. I could tell Boss Rowley was nervous about slipping on all the water. After all, Boss Rowley is seventy-five and I am sixty-three.

Rowley remarked to Jay, "The water hose is loose and is spraying out water."

Early this morning, as Mr. Rowley took Bo and me into the lobby of our building, I saw Anthony, our doorman, and Jane, who lives on the sixth floor, approaching us. Jane was being led by Dixie, her small dog of indescribable breed with black and white markings. Bo ran forward and kissed Dixie. I was not jealous, even though Bo spends a lot of time kissing my face, eyes, and ears.

"Good morning, Jane. Good morning, Dixie. Good morning, Anthony."

"Good morning, Mr. Rowley."

"They're two beautiful dogs," said Jane.

"They were washed and groomed yesterday. I was, too," replied Peter Rowley.

"You're beautiful, too."

The boss stayed silent. Jane had to be referring to me! It's true. I don't deny it! I've come a long way from South Jersey.

It had rained heavily in the mountains of the northern Catskills. You would think that by now, that incompetent Mr. Rowley knows I have trouble with big steps. The steps to the kitchen in the rear of the Onteora house are few and large. It so happened that Bo and I had had a peaceful night, although Mr. and Mrs. Rowley had argued the evening before. About what I don't know and don't care. Maybe it was Bo's incontinence? Humans are so childish.

At any rate, the back staircase consists of a few big steps covered by a yellowish faded carpet. It was used by the maid and cook in the 1920s. I suppose witless Rowley thought the front steps that were not as high and were more numerous were better for me. We reached the top of the staircase, that idiot Rowley half-asleep pulling us both along. Bo suddenly scrambled down the stairs and was gone like a rocket, but I slipped on the top step and slid on my side all the way down thirteen steps to a landing where there was a gray carpet. Mr. Rowley shouted, "Oh, my God!" A lot of good that did!

Mrs. Rowley came running out in her nightgown. "Amelia, are you all right?! Darling!" she screamed.

I rolled over, picked myself up, and walked on all four legs down the bottom four steps from the landing. So it goes!

That Rowley is such a moron! I managed to really pull off a graceful slide. I was impressed with my skill!

Then Bo suddenly runs pell-mell, leaping above the oriental carpet, landing on my side, and biting my ear. I snarl. We whirl around while I manage to deftly maneuver my larger body faster than Bo thought possible. Barks. Snarls. Tumbling over each other.

This continues for a minute or two. Bo and I are playfully furious. I have become entangled with a whirling dervish.

Back in the city, I did not like the repairman working on the Rowleys' ovens and did my best to bite him. He said, "If you don't take that dog away, I'm leaving."

Mrs. Rowley and her friend, Vimila, an Indian opera singer, put up the gate across the opening of the kitchen door.

Later that day, I overheard Mr. Rowley tell Caroline, "This morning, I went to Chelsea Piers to play golf. All of a sudden, as the other golfers and I were shooting balls out onto the pier, a white seagull flew inside the high netting. He or she landed at the far end near the two-hundred-yard sign beyond which is the Hudson River. It was a sunny cold day. There was an announcement over a loudspeaker telling us to stop hitting golf balls. Four employees stepped onto the pier and walked slowly toward the bird. It tried to fly out but kept hitting the nets. The gull grew tired and landed on top of a pile of netting on the far right near the river. A woman employee approached the bird, waving a white cloth, but she could not reach the creature which remained a couple of feet above her. Then whoever was running the rescue directed that the nets around three of the four sides of the pier be electrically lowered. Jonathan Seagull flew away."

After Mr. Rowley returned from his latest trip to England—and once again, he never asked my permission to go—he told me that his housekeepers at Morcott Hall, Sandra and Ian I'Anson, said that they were afraid the pet pheasant which they and the boss had cared for last summer had been shot by a hunter during the current hunting season or murdered by a villager or some visitor to the area. The pheasant was so tame that it might have casually approached someone who could have then strangled it for both the fun of it and to provide his or her dinner. Mr. Rowley actually has a friend who strangled a cock pheasant because it was threatening his wife.

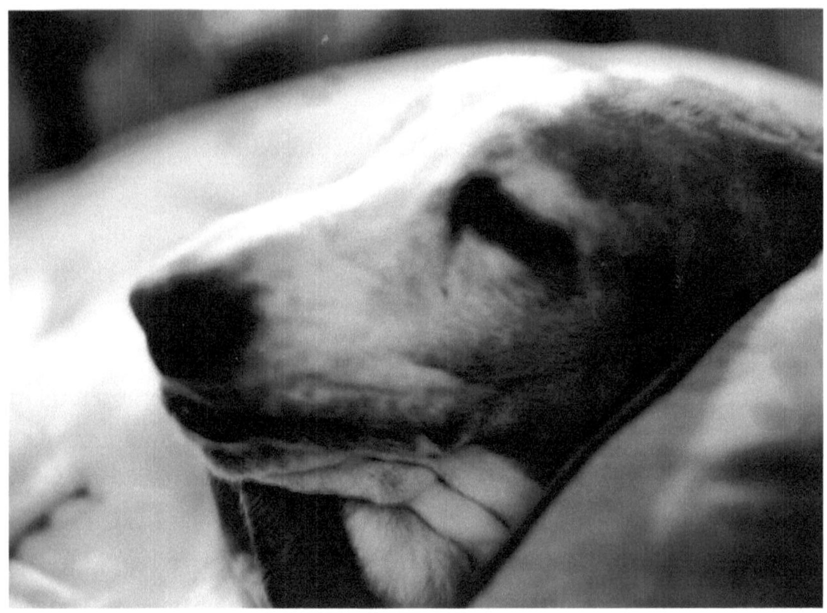

I went to Harvard. That's a lie.

However, said the I'Ansons, Attila, the baby pheasant's father, had invited into the grounds five young male pheasants. Mr. Rowley thought this unusual as pheasants are territorial. The very next day, Rowley was having breakfast looking out the window at the garden when a very young pheasant walked slowly across the grass of the lawn, then over the gravel of the drive, and finally up the narrow stone paving that borders the front of the house. Rowley thought the pheasant was about the size the baby would now be since he hadn't seen it since last summer and it would have grown. He realized that the pet pheasant had survived and was visiting the home of its earliest days. Mr. Rowley was very careful not to make a move, and after a while, he peeked around the corner of another window but could no longer see the bird. I'm glad the baby pheasant hadn't died as I dislike humans killing any of my fellow creatures, whether pigs, deer, cattle, birds, or bassets.

I'm personally not very keen on birds, but I like to chase them, though I've never caught one. My best chance is with the pigeons on Park Avenue and in Central Park.

Mr. Rowley told me another story about birds at his English house. The crow had been regularly attacking the skylight windows above his top-floor office. "Bang, bang!" with his beak. Then he would fly away. Rowley thought at first the crow resented Rowley occupying his office, but then when Rowley was somewhere else in the house, the crow would attack the same windows again. Or perhaps the crow just liked the noise he made and the opportunity to exercise his beak!

I'm glad the crow can't assault me because I'd show him a thing or two with my bark and bite if I were over there, which I don't really expect to happen. Even though the Brits wouldn't quarantine me for six months the way they used to, I would still be punctured with shots and forced to fly in the hold of the plane instead of with my dear Rowleys.

Meanwhile, back at the ranch, what was going on with yours truly? The Rowleys abandoned me to go first to Nassau in the Caribbean (no, not Queens, God forbid, where no Park Avenue dog should ever have to go) and then to England. I was informed that this time I would be put in the gentle care of Pat McGregor. Bo and I would go together, and we would spend happy days in Pat's West Side apartment—a chance for Bo to learn a new and better set of bathroom habits.

However, the Rowleys were shocked three weeks later when I was returned alone to 815 without my best friend Bo. Mrs. Rowley exclaimed, "Peter, come quick! Look at Amelia!"

I smelled. My odor, which even bothered me (and I am not

persnickety), was stronger than it had ever been. I had spent the last three weeks at Pat McGregor's Woodstock farm, where I was never washed. I had a longish black streak under my chin, and both my eyes were surrounded by black patches. Before I could say *basset hound*, I found myself in the Rowley's master bath being soaped and washed by Avra, the vet, and her assistant.

The next day, I heard Mrs. Rowley demanding an explanation from the woman who runs Pat's Woodstock farm. "We didn't bathe her because we didn't want her to catch cold, and we didn't want her to tire her weak rear legs by walking too much," said the woman. Later, I heard Mrs. Rowley giving Pat an earful.

However, a day after all the excitement, I overheard Mrs. Rowley say to her husband, "I will say this. Amelia's weight is perfect. But Pat's going to train Bo for two more weeks free of charge."

About two weeks after I returned from Pat's, the boss took me downstairs rather early, as usual. For some reason, he had me on a looser leash. I saw the two black Scotties approaching from the opposite direction. Did Rowley think I was suddenly feeling friendly toward my two enemies, or was he looking for a fight? I leapt. The Scottie closest to me leapt at the same time. My jaw was open, my teeth bared. Our jaws met, and we both snarled. What a glorious morning!

Matthew, Mr. Rowley's brilliant computer guru, arrived an hour later, and they transferred the boss' story about the English birds from his desktop to the laptop. However, they forgot that Rowley's account of my smelly adventure with Pat and her farm manager was also on the laptop. When the laptop said, "Do you want to replace your earlier file with the current one?" or words to that effect (I am not very computer literate), they said "Yes."

All of Mr. Rowley's moving story of my life with Pat was gone, and Matthew frantically tried to retrieve it from outer space to no avail. So Mr. Rowley promptly summoned the services of John Pieza, Mrs. Rowley's computer consultant. John and Rowley-poly discovered the font size was different on the English bird passages, and this was apparently affecting Mr. Rowley's reconstruction of his deathless words about me and Pat.

It's been some two weeks that I noticed that Boss Rowley began to walk rather strangely. He started hugging the side of the hall when taking me outside. He seemed nervous that I might pull him over. Perish the thought—though it would be sweet revenge for all the times he's pulled me by the neck. Then he stopped taking me out altogether. Instead, Mrs. Rowley started taking me out on my bathroom breaks, and most amazing of all, Caroline took me out this morning!

I heard Mr. Rowley say last night, "I'm tired after having two MRIs taken of my back." I notice Boss Rowley moves very slowly around the apartment. Suddenly, he walks like an old man. Well, at seventy-five, maybe he is an old cuss. I felt sorry for him, so after Caroline brought me back to my apartment, I wandered over to where Rowley was having breakfast. He called, "Amelia," and I went and lay down beside his chair, and he stroked me. I hope he lives as long as me!

Then last night, I detected panic in Mrs. Rowley's sweet Hungarian-accented voice. "Amelia's got a big bump above her right hip!"

Of course I do. I already know that, and it worries me because it's above my right leg, which is weaker than my left leg, and the main reason I had had a disc operation on my back early last summer.

"I'll have to call the vet today," added Mrs. Rowley. Maybe I won't live as long as Mr. Rowley! A pity! The rat! But what can you expect of a human? All humans live longer than we do. Very unfair. Bassets are the No. 1 species in the world and should live longer than anyone else, n'est-ce pas?

This morning Mr. Rowley put the collar around my neck, and, after he threatened to lift the edge of my round bed, I got up and waddled normally into the kitchen. The boss said to his wife, "She walked okay this morning." I may live longer!! Hooray!! Let's see how Rowley himself walks today!

I'm really becoming used to Mrs. Rowley taking me instead of the slow-moving Mr. Rowley. Do I like her technique better than his? Yes and no. He pulls one way, she pulls another. She calls me "ami." He calls me "hound-dog," and as I wrote earlier, sings that Elvis Presley song in an unspeakably off-key voice that would make any other basset cringe—something I just have to put up with, and my long ears are no help. So it goes.

Shocking news! It happened yesterday, and I must say it frightened me. Cancer! Avra the vet and her female assistant held me tight while one of them stuck a needle into my small growth.

"It may be benign," said Avra.

I hope so. Last night, I overheard Terez saying to Peter, "I couldn't stand it if Amelia dies!" I feel the same way! We shall see. Didn't Queen Victoria always speak in the third person?

A friend of the boss came into my apartment: a kindly elderly man with white hair, a little plump. Rowley said, "There's a cancer scare—a growth on her hip." The visitor said, "They often have cephalus growths." I was glad to hear that!

Letitia's gone, by the way. At least for now. Blood was pouring out of her, and blood was being poured into her, though I never saw any of this. Poor woman. I love her. There was something about a magic pill with a camera inside. Could she afford it? I hope so.

Now I have a new walker, Sheila. She's English, elegant, and pretty. She pleads with me in a little soft soprano voice to move. Of course I don't.

But eventually I do.

That Bo—that seventeen pounds of insolent young black fuzzy furry dog—races after a small red rubber ball thrown by Lady Rowley as I lie upside down watching him. Why is he here this weekend?! Can't a woman have any peace? He's so young, and I'm so old.

I overheard Mr. Rowley say, "I prefer Sheila to Letitia." Mr. Rowley went on, "But we have to give Letitia her job back. I don't know how long she's going to be with us, though."

Mrs. Rowley said, "Letitia smokes nonstop."

What a shock I got this morning! There I was minding my business in the kitchen sleeping on my multicolored brocade bed waiting for someone to take me out—I tell you it's a challenge holding back my poo-poo and pee-pee for ten hours—when there was this terrific clatter. All these pewter silver trays, as well as a wooden one, suddenly slid off the top of the refrigerator and crashed to the kitchen floor while old Rowley was making coffee! I thought the world had come to an end! Then he said to me, after he'd picked up the four silver dishes and the wooden one, "I was shocked too, Amelia." He stroked me on my head. What a jerk. But I like him.

Letitia is miraculously back from the dead and now feeding me. She leans her head down, and I manage to raise my long head and kiss her on the lips!

I had let out a long, loud groan in my sleep at six this morning. I was dreaming of Bo being eaten by a cat. I should be so lucky!

How dare he! The boss came in this morning at eight and in the dark as I was continuing my early morning snooze and then stepped on my tail! Fortunately, he was wearing his soft white furry slippers. And I still love him. I knew he wanted me to walk into the kitchen. I did so, but I took my time. I have some pride. Bo was still there. I only wish the cat had been real! Pat McGregor's assistant had forgotten to pick up Bo. It was raining cats and dogs.

I overheard a long discussion in midmorning between Mrs. Rowley and Pat McGregor, the dog trainer, regarding Bo's bathroom habits (or lack thereof). Pat did most of the talking. They can't complain about me! They should have seen me on the O'Dell farmstead, but that was a long time ago and not a good memory. I'm a well-trained Park Avenue dog now.

Mrs. Rowley said to Letitia in midafternoon, "Amelia's only to be taken out wearing a harness. Otherwise, we'll break her neck, pulling her." I certainly agree with that. Still, my neck's pretty strong. Over nine years, I've resisted being told what to do! You would, too, if you were me. Long live all basset hounds! We may have floppy ears, but we're smarter than anyone else on this planet. And in truth, I do have a very nice disposition to boot. I rarely bark. Everyone says, "Amelia's so sweet."

Mr. Rowley gently pulls my big new cushion with the red, brown, and gold brocade fabric. Sometimes I sleep on it rather than on my other two beds—the gray one and the dark brown one. I heard Caroline say, "They smell!" So they're being cleaned. But to get back to Mr. Rowley tugging on my beautiful brocade one, I knew this was the signal he wanted me to get up and leave my position beside my mistress's sleeping form on the Rowleys' king-sized bed. I lumber into the kitchen. He walks behind me with the brocade mattress and carefully positions it on the floor a few feet from the back door near the stove. I will be able to sleep there, and it is beside my metal water bowl. I am very happy.

Mr. Rowley shuts both doors quietly.

Lo and behold, Pat McGregor opens the back door one morning and just takes me away. I shall miss the Rowleys. I knew they were going on a vacation to Chile with a stop in Sao Paulo so Mr. Rowley could visit Embraer, an aerospace company that makes business jets. I wish he would take me on one. I would promise I wouldn't go to the bathroom on an executive jet carpet, though it should be called a Basset Jet.

One week later, and the horrible Rowleys have returned from their Chile/Brazil jaunt. I, too, have returned to 815 Park, where I don't hesitate to express my feelings about my involuntary exile in ways that can only be described to my more delicate readers as exercising my right to freely indulge in natural functions. For this, I was banished to the kitchen all night, and today the terrifying vet, Avra, and her assistant came to see me. I know Mrs. Rowley refused to look at what they were doing to me.

I won't tell you what I did in the Rowley's bedroom the night before last, but I heard the boss say to her ladyship, "There was a horrible smell all night."

"I know."

"I picked it up this morning, and apparently, I dropped a blob on the cabinet in front of the DVD player. This evening, I thought it was chocolate until I touched it. Ugh. That explains the horrible odor all day."

Never cross a basset hound by going off to South America without taking her!

No more Bo. I miss him. But he had been a bad dog! Things coming out of him that should not come out of a Park Avenue dog. I suppose up in Harlem, they might not object so much, although that's a politically incorrect thing to write, but I don't think he'd be popular there either. And then he'd be sent to the pound, and we all know what happens to dogs in the pound—even bassets—unless they are rescued.

Letitia said, “What is she thinking about?”

I was staring into outer space, refusing to eat my bowl of dinner.

“Does she think about Chile?”

Of course, I’m concerned whether any basset hounds were hurt in the earthquakes there. Can you see their ears sticking out above the rubble?

Early this morning, I let out two loud groans that sounded more like roars. I’ll have to go to a psychiatrist. I was having a bad dream.

Bo is back! He turned up yesterday, and I was rather cold toward him when we were taken out. Today, however, we played outside. He’s a changed dog. Previously, he used to run around at full speed, leaving nasty little messes. I think Letitia kept him locked up all day and night in her one-room apartment. But now he’s calmer and friendlier. He’s even polite. I remember hearing that’s what happened with their orange marmalade-colored cat, Tilly. The Rowleys put her in the care of their previous maid, Encarnita, for the summer, and she kept her locked up day and night in a dirty garage. When she returned to the Rowleys, she ignored her litter box, and the Rowleys had to give her away.

I sleep all night and most of the day. I have always slept most of the day because there’s nothing else to do once I’ve been fully fed by the Rowleys. There are no dogs or rabbits to chase and there is no food to be found. But now, I sleep most of the day because I’m old. But don’t think I’m not still alert, and don’t think I can’t still run. My ears still move and my eyebrows rise whenever Boss Rowley says “Amelia” or “hound dog.” When the Rowleys tell me to go to the bedroom to climb on my big round pillow decorated with patterns and covered with a white blanket trimmed with ribbon on the edge, I bound along as usual, ears flapping, rear legs swinging side to side. And Bo follows me, even though he can go much faster than me.

That weekend, it was raining cats and dogs. Leticia was shoving a pill down my throat, as I wouldn't eat. She always tries to trick me into swallowing a pill along with a mouthful of whatever they call my chow. Anyway, out I went, and of course, I got very wet. To her full credit, Letitia did dry me off later with a nice clean white towel.

Caroline's birthday, her twenty-eighth. Everybody forgot to take me and Bo out this misty morning when the clocks change to summertime, but then Pat McGregor arrives to take Bo away. She sees me, dying to go out. So she takes me along with Bo, and I run happily to keep up with him. Then she brings me back, and I feel much better and settle in for a morning snooze until Letitia arrives. Why didn't Sheila come to take me out this morning? Sheila's my new part-time dog walker. But Sheila hasn't picked up the envelope with the money she's already earned. Mrs. Rowley has been quite mystified. But it didn't worry me. I'm always glad to keep my money.

Wouldn't you know it! This morning, Sheila dropped by. She took her money but never opened the kitchen door to the dining room. Of course, as I don't talk, Mr. Rowley can't tell whether I went outside or not when I am lying there on my cushion.

Bo was a very bad dog last night. Mr. Rowley stepped in his poo-poo, which Bo had cleverly hidden by leaving it on the brown narrow board separating the so-called new room from the dining room. The master was not pleased. The boss spent a long time cleaning his shoes in the bathroom, using toilet paper, tissues, water, and even a paper clip.

Bo had also struck with Nos. 1 and 2 in all sorts of places all over the apartment. Mrs. Rowley said to Mr. Rowley, "It got onto our shoes, and we must have carried it everywhere." Mrs. Rowley spent three hours on her hands and knees cleaning, scraping and scrubbing.

"That dog is going!" she said.

After three days of rain, the sun is finally shining. Bo was still here early this morning when Pat's girl picked him up, but I'm afraid his days may be numbered. Mrs. Rowley said, "The phone keeps ringing, and I have contractors coming. And I'm feeling guilty about sending Bo away."

It's St. Patrick's Day, and Bo has been banished. Will he ever come back?

More excitement! Mr. Rowley assumed Sheila had forgotten to take me out and called Letitia, who rushed over, but then Mr. Rowley told my mistress that perhaps Sheila had come but had just not opened the door from the kitchen to the dining room.

Then I heard the boss ask Mrs. Rowley, who is the real boss, whether we could give Bo another chance. Mrs. Rowley replied that perhaps he did not fully appreciate what it was like to spend three hours cleaning up after my friend. Mr. Rowley said he was sorry.

Last night, Peter put me in the kitchen. I waited. I heard him call Sheila. "Don't forget to take Amelia out. Please phone when you get this message." Sheila finally phoned.

Mrs. Rowley said to Peter in their bedroom, "Where is my darling Amelia? Leave all the doors open in this part of the apartment so she can come in after Sheila brings her back."

Peter appeared in my kitchen, but there was no sign of Sheila.

Then Mrs. Rowley said, "Sheila said she was going to a reception." At ten o'clock, the boss, wearing his pajamas, came into my kitchen looking for me and saw Sheila taking off my collar. Sheila looked up, "I can't get Amelia to go out the door into the dining room."

The boss said, "I'll persuade her." He opened the door into his little office, and I happily loped to the bedroom to snuggle up on my big embroidered cushion next to the lady of the house.

Bo's exile continues. After I go out, I lie on the oriental rug, which used to be my surreptitious bathroom and is Bo's now. Then Peter calls, "Amelia." I look up. He waves a hand to say hello, fluttering his fingers. After a while, I go and lie in a patch of sun in another place on the beautiful carpet.

Yesterday was the first day of spring; it was almost as nice and sunny as the day before. The Rowleys disappeared in the midmorning and returned in the late afternoon. Sheila took me out at night, and after I returned I walked down to their bedroom. The door was only partly open. Perhaps I am naturally cautious or because I am stubborn, I refused to push it open and stood there on all four paws. Bo would have pushed it wide. Maybe I'm extra careful because of my childhood experience with the O'Dells. Then Peter got out of bed and opened the door and I lay down on the floor beside Mrs. Rowley.

Today, it's raining. Letitia told the Rowleys that I whined and barked a long time after they had left on their Sunday outing. Letitia said, "After I left Amelia, I could still hear her downstairs."

I heard Mrs. Rowley say yesterday, "I just can't have Bo back. And I can't keep on paying for him at Pat's. I wish he was white rather than black."

Mr. Rowley passed me by a couple of times saying, "crazy dog," "crazy hound dog" or "hound dog." I pay no attention.

I heard Mrs. Rowley complaining to Pat's accountant about her bill for Bo. She is young and Chinese, "I can't fax you because you gave me the wrong phone number. I can't phone you because you won't answer or the line is always busy."

Mrs. Rowley said to Mr. Rowley, "Will you phone Pat? She'll listen to you." The boss left a message on Pat's answering machine.

The Chinese woman called back right away. Mrs. Rowley told

her she couldn't understand the weekly and monthly charges. Mrs. Rowley added, "I'm telling American Express not to pay any more bills from you."

Then I knew Bo was gone for good.

Mrs. Rowley turned to Peter, "Will Amelia miss her?"

"I don't know."

"Pat owes me a lot of money as she promised she wouldn't charge me for the mess that she returned Amelia in last November--dirty ears, eye infection, unwashed body."

I am now three pounds overweight, and I need dental care. I heard I'm to go to Oradell Hospital while the Rowleys are in England.

I wish Bo good luck.

NO MORE BO

I like Oradell.

Well, I'm not sure I *like* Oradell. Without telling me, they make me go to sleep. The next thing I know, I'm missing six teeth! Anyway, I'm back home with the Rowleys who have returned from England, and Mr. Rowley is telling me about the oversexed pheasant at Morcott Hall. At least Attila's behavior is a distraction from my toothache. Rowley says he makes this wild mating call every two or three minutes, particularly in the morning. He flaps his wings gently—I guess to warm up the muscles. Then he emits this roar and flaps his wings furiously, and he hopes a lady friend will fly over the garden wall.

Mr. Rowley says he watched him one afternoon following his girlfriend (Attila's girlfriend, not Mr. Rowley's—Mr. Rowley doesn't have a girlfriend) who was eating bugs in a flower bed. Mr. Rowley says he never saw Attila jump on the female, but I guess that's what Attila really wanted to do. Rowley also says Attila sometimes has two lady friends in the garden. So I guess group sex keeps him busy, leaping from the back of one to the other. Ah, love. It's spring.

My mouth is still sore, and I've now decided that I don't ever want to return to Oradell!

Letitia says, "If I don't kiss Amelia on her lips before she eats, she looks up at me expectantly, and she won't eat until I do."

One night, Caroline left the door to Mr. Rowley's office open while I was locked in the kitchen. I was waiting for Sheila, who takes me out for my nightly bathroom stroll. So I walked into the Rowleys' bedroom and went to sleep on one of my beds. I guess Mr. Rowley must have thought Sheila had taken me out, seeing me wander by on the floor below him.

About half an hour later, Caroline lets out a scream from her bedroom. "There's someone in the apartment!" It turns out to be Sheila looking for me. Mr. and Mrs. Rowley rush out—he in his pajamas, and she in her nightgown.

After Sheila brought me back from our walk, I opted to sleep in the living room on my most expensive bed, but during the night, I got my revenge on the Rowleys for their earlier confusion by doing No. 2 on the dining room carpet.

Sheila said, "I think Amelia misses Bo. When he sees this little white dog on Seventy-Fifth Street, he whimpers."

I notice Letitia has the smell of another dog on her. Letitia admits to Mr. Rowley and me, "I'm walking a little white dog on the sixth floor." I'm jealous. Even though Letitia kisses me on the lips, I refuse to eat my morning meal.

I notice out of the corner of my eye Mr. Rowley watching Letitia and me as he leans on the marble counter of the kitchen table. What else can you expect of a shifty writer surreptitiously writing a book about me? He thinks I don't know, but I do.

"It's a job you've taken?" says the boss.

"Yes. Only two days ago."

"It's a little dog like Bo?"

"Yes. It's a French bulldog called Tallulah." Letitia gestures with her hands to show how small it is. She puts the collar around my neck.

I stop being jealous and start to eat my food.

Nevertheless, when I see Tallulah, I growl.

It's 11:30 p.m. I don't see him, but I sense that Mr. Rowley has woken up, come out to the hall, and expects me to come to the Rowleys' bedroom. I pad softly toward the bedroom through the open door of the hallway to my nesting place next to Mrs. Rowley.

Rowley claps his hands, says, "Chop-chop." I get up. He waves with his hands for me to go to the kitchen. I do.

The next week, I suffer another insult to my dignity! At the vet's office, John Pieza, who Mr. Rowley calls "Pizza" behind his back, picked me up and then stood on the new high-tech bathroom scales. I heard him say to Rowley, "Fifty-six point eight pounds."

I know they want me to lose weight, which I don't really like to do, but I certainly don't want to have another disc removal operation followed by recuperation in the Oradell Animal Hospital. I know Mr. Rowley suspects Letitia of feeding me hot dogs, cookies, and gumdrops to make me move when I go outside.

Rowley, Rowley! How many times have I told him to stay away from very big dogs—giant dogs. Who can forget the time a few years ago when that enormous dog two doors away frightened me and I bayed like a basset hound, causing an embarrassed Mr. Rowley to tell me to shush. This was just not done on Park Avenue.

But now Boss Rowley goes to stay with some friends in a neighboring state and gets scratched by a 125-pound schnauzer while swimming in his host's pool. Boss Rowley is recovering from back trouble and was probably swimming for therapeutic reasons as much as for pleasure. The schnauzer, whose name was Fritz, was not supposed to be in the pool. But he broke the house rules, and while Peter Rowley floundered around in the middle of the pool looking for shallower footing, the schnauzer affectionately scratched his left arm and tried to paw his stomach. Fortunately, at that moment, Rowley found a spot where he could stand in the pool and fend off the disobedient dog.

Fritz, Rowley told me, climbed with some difficulty out of the stone-lined pool, black stringy hair soaking wet, and trotted happily back to his owner's Colonial gingerbread manor. The boss said he asked his hostess an hour or so later to lend him some disinfectant, which he sprayed on the red streak. Will he sue his host and hostess? I don't think so, as he likes them, and because they had organized a very successful trip to Chile for Mr. and Mrs. Rowley and some other friends.

It's the longest day of the year, but Rowley still hasn't learned to treat me with the respect that I and other bassets around the world deserve. Usually when he sees me, when he passes by me, walking properly or with a slight limp, caused by his back trouble, he cries, "Crazy dog." I am usually lying there doing nothing, eyeing him in his fruitless pursuit of fame, money, or whatever. I know he says it with affection, but I am not nuts. I am just a basset with long floppy ears and a unique way of walking and a very independent disposition. "Crazy dog."

People may think I'm stupid or uncooperative because I refuse to go faster when Letitia is trying to persuade me to speed up on the sidewalk, but when it comes to crossing the street, I manage to accelerate quite rapidly until I reach the pavement on the other side of the street.

Mr. Rowley tells me the latest about Attila, the pheasant with a harem, from what he observed in England this summer. Attila has a wife, but whether it's the same one as last year I do not know. I do not pry. Attila's lady friend is yellow and gray and probably lives in a bush. Attila walks around his property as usual, eating grass and insects on the lawns. At 5:30 in the morning, he goes on a tour of Morcott Hall grounds, which all belong to him, not the Rowleys

(I'm sure he thinks), and crawls under a hole in the tennis court wiring. Early one morning, Boss Rowley saw a magpie—a beautiful black and white bird—land on the front lawn. Magpies like to eat other birds' eggs. I hope he doesn't find Attila's wife's eggs.

Yesterday, Rowley allowed a lady called Trish into my kitchen where I was snoozing, minding my own business. Trish is the co-owner of a contracting company, which is renovating the Rowleys' new studio on the floor above. I wonder if they'll let me in there. Basset hounds have a right to studios like everyone else. She says to Rowley, "Do you think I can pet her?" meaning me.

"Sure," says the boss.

She leans toward me, extending a hand. I growl softly. "Guess not," says Trish. "When I see her outside, she's friendly."

"I'm sorry," says the boss.

It's my first trip to Low-Cost Valley, i.e., Locust Valley. Mrs. Rowley, Caroline, and Peter took me so I could put on a show for a big dinner party that they were giving in the summer house Caroline was renting. There were to be twenty-seven guests served by a staff of three. I wandered around among the legs, sniffing grass and shoes. People remarked on my brown and white coat. Of course, they wanted to stroke me, but they're a little careful about that because they don't know if I might bite their ankles. I smelled the filet mignon. Then they shut me up in the senior Rowleys' bedroom during dinner.

At about eleven o'clock, I began to whine, so out I came into the living room. Most of the people had gone.

At 7:30 the next morning, Rowley took me for a walk. Upon our return, a dog across the street started to bark and charge toward me and Rowley, so we quickly retreated up the steps. Rowley opened the glass door, and with difficulty, I climbed up and got inside just in time. My hind legs have been bothering me. On the trip back to the city, I slept between the Rowleys on the rear seat in my nice comfortable small oval bed covered with a blanket. Mrs. Rowley caressed my haunches and Peter my head, although I must say he pushed me away a number of times, which I did not like. He was trying to read the British satirical magazine, *Private Eye*.

It was about ten o'clock, and I'm lying there in the kitchen, waiting for Sheila to come to take me out. Rowley passes by. I sense Sheila is coming. It's my ESP. I get up from my round pouf in the living room and amble toward the kitchen. Sheila opens the kitchen door and comes in. Out of the corner of my eye, I see Rowley in his office. Rowley says to Sheila, "Amelia knew you were coming and got up before you opened the kitchen door."

Rowley is really disgusting. He pretends to love animals and me, and there he goes this morning frying bacon and bread, his favorite British breakfast. I can smell it! I can hear it frying in the pan and see him standing above the stove. Once again, I'm lying there in the kitchen waiting to be taken out by Sheila. Think of the poor piggy. It does smell pretty good, though—better than anything I got in South Jersey.

Well, well, well. I was having a good time eating more than usual the last few weeks. One of my favorites was a little cookie that was good for my teeth. My bosses (i.e., Terez and Peter Rowley, and their doctors or vets—whatever they call themselves and I don't like them) said there was stuff in these special snacks that would coat my teeth so they wouldn't fall out. Anyway to my horror, they're taking away my lovely delicacies.

I heard Mrs. Rowley say, "The doctors say she's putting on weight. Amelia has gained three pounds since last June." Mrs. Rowley's voice rose to a higher pitch. What's three pounds? I only weighed fifty-six point eight then, and now I am fifty-nine point five. It's very unfair. And to top it all off, they've pasted the diet in the little book, titled Amelia's Diet Schedule.

I won't bore you with all the contents, but listen to this:

"Nine o'clock: Early-morning walk
Two o'clock: Science Diet Light - Adult Small Biscuits
Four o'clock: Early-evening walk
1/3 cup of dry food - W/D low-fat
AND
¼ cup of wet food - W/D Hill's Prescription Diet in can"

The *in can* was in ink and in Mrs. Rowley's handwriting.

After Sheila leaves me at about eleven, I pad down the long dark corridor and into the Rowleys' bedroom where I nestle down on my big bed. Sometimes I sleep on my right side.

It was about a quarter to eleven when the phone suddenly rang. A man's voice, neither angry nor happy, mentioned the word *dog* on the answering machine. The Rowleys were half-asleep in their king-sized bed. Rowley had just been down to the kitchen and had noticed the leash was gone and concluded I was out with Sheila. He thought nothing of it and climbed back into bed. But the phone call set off alarm bells in both Rowleys. Was Amelia injured? Had she died in a car accident? And what about Sheila? The Rowleys discussed how Sheila would take out Amelia so late every night.

Mr. Rowley suggested to Mrs. Rowley that Sheila not be allowed to take me down a certain side street. Did Sheila meet men who stopped to comment on my beauty or funny shape and ears (take your pick)? Mrs. Rowley guessed Sheila had been married twice. Were they even safe on Park Avenue? Peter thought Amelia would bite the ankles of any man who attacked Sheila, but would Amelia always frighten the rapist away? Peter phoned Steve, the big doorman, who said, "Sheila went out with Amelia ten minutes ago." How long ago was ten minutes, the Rowleys wondered? Was it longer? The Rowleys discussed the sound of the man's voice. How had he got Mrs. Rowley's phone number?

Peter tried to sooth my mistress, and, though admitting he was worried, said of the message, "It's a mystery." Peter added he had seen Sheila elegantly dressed on another evening on Park Avenue. She was always well-dressed. They both knew she liked to go to art gallery openings. Mrs. Rowley phoned Steve. He said, "I can see Sheila on the other side of the avenue with the dog." Mrs. Rowley relayed this to Peter. They both breathed a sigh of relief. About three minutes later, I walked into Mr. Rowley's office from the kitchen on the way to their bedroom. Mr. Rowley exclaimed, "She's here!"

Now I'm feeling lonely. It's also very hot outside: ninety-five degrees. I whine. I continue whining. Then Peter, who is reading an English newspaper, says, slapping his thigh, "Come here, Amelia." I ignore this. I continue whining in my special blend of bass and tenor sounds. Rowley slaps his thigh several times, repeating, "Come here, Amelia." I get up, walk over, and sit down beside his leg. He starts to stroke my back and then gently kneads my neck. I lie on my side against his leg, and he continues the stroking, this time the side of my white chest. I look up, and he fondles my neck.

Mrs. Rowley, or my darling Terez, was ticked at Sheila for not taking me out until about eleven (I'm not sure of the time as I'm not very good at telling time; I only know when it's time to eat, sleep, piss, or shit—sorry, urinate or defecate; as a Park Avenue dog, I have to be careful about my language), and twice I went to their bedroom only to be taken back to the kitchen to await Sheila's return from her habitual nocturnal entertainment. As a result, Terez read Sheila the riot act over the phone about how she had to take me out by nine-thirty ("You're being cruel to the dog,") or she,

Terez, would have to go outside with me. Even the boss had phoned Sheila, but his voice was calmer and probably less persuasive; in fact, he had made the first call to Sheila, leaving a message on her cell phone.

Terez kisses me.

Today, I learned that the Rowleys had had to pay Mrs. Amanda Haynes-Dale about $1,200 for alleged damage to her twelfth floor apartment on the B line (I live on the C line). This was all apparently due to the Rowleys' contractors using an electric jackhammer while restoring the studio on the penthouse, i.e., the sixteenth floor, which the Rowleys bought on the other side of 815 Park above the A line. The Rowleys were not happy about having to pay Amanda, whom they have never met in person, but their lawyer, John Gerhard, of Cravath, Swaine, and Moore (a very expensive law firm), advised them to, averting Amanda's small claims action against them. No doubt John Gerhard's bill will exceed Amanda's damages, but the boss had made clear to Mrs. Rowley, "They're a first-class law firm, and I don't want any more trouble from Amanda." Of course, Cravath never handles small claims cases, but as a favor to the boss, they advised him to settle with Amanda.

So this morning when Letitia was returning me to 815 Park, I saw Amanda under the awning and charged her, trying to bite her ankle, but Letitia held me back. How did I know it was the Rowleys' enemy? I just did. Mrs. Rowley gave Marcel, one of my favorite doormen who's in charge of the front door on weekdays, twenty dollars not to tell Amanda who owned me!

Marcel, our dauntless doorman, later told Mr. Rowley I did not try to bite Amanda but that rather when Amanda bent down to stroke me, she suddenly jumped back as if I had snapped at her, but I hadn't.

I had never done this before, but I had to take action when Rowley, who I guessed was reading the Sunday *New York Times* by the window above the synagogue, failed to take me out of the bedroom at eight o'clock! I let out a bark. Nothing happened, so after two seconds, I barked again. Rowley, abandoning his paper on the last page of the style section, hurried in. I jogged to the kitchen. Mrs. Rowley, who the night before had told Mr. Rowley he was an uncaring husband, was sound asleep. A little later, Mrs. Rowley awoke and apologized to him for her remarks. He said, "That's okay." Mrs. Rowley had been working hard all day on paying bills and had slept little the night before that. Her arthritis was bothering her.

I had heard another dog was going to visit me that evening. Cathy Michaelson, the dog's owner, said, "I didn't bring him because I wanted a rest. He's only a year and a half old and runs and jumps all the time." I was disappointed. Then the boss took me by the elevator to Caroline's penthouse, and I started to whine. Cathy, who Mr. Rowley was showing the new penthouse to, said,

"Amelia's ill. Look at how her stomach is bloated. She's full of gas." I continued to whine. Rowley hurried down the spiral staircase, calling, "Terez. Come quick. Amelia's ill. Cathy says we'll have to take her to the vet." Mrs. Rowley arrived. I curled up beside her feet and stopped whining.

The following morning, I see the boss carrying his tray of breakfast food, which he does not offer me, to his chair above the synagogue, having played early morning tennis against Jerry Hurwitz. He looks happy because the score was a tie and Hurwitz usually wins. I wander in, looking for company. He says, "Good morning, Amelia." I settle down in a patch of sun on the oriental carpet and parquet floor near him.

The very next day, the boss was trying to hurry me along so that I would eat my food and go out with Letitia.

Letitia said, "She's dragging her right foot."

The boss said, "I notice in the early morning that's the weak one when she gets up."

"She's getting older," Letitia said.

As if I didn't know!

Meanwhile, I've been noticing the boss has been getting weaker on his right side and sometimes seems to limp. Not really surprising, given that he's seventy-six years old, which is about the same age as me, if you use that human calculation of seven times a dog's age, making me older than seventy. Which of us will die first? We'll see, although unfortunately basset hounds do not live as long as humans, which seems unfair. Oh well. That's life.

Sheila brings me back up the back elevator, and I overhear her and the boss, "Good morning, Sheila."

This surprises me as I know he doesn't like to talk to her in the morning, and Mrs. Rowley feels the same way. Sheila likes to talk and talk.

Goodbye, cruel world.

"Good morning, Peter. It's a beautiful day. You should go outside."

The boss can obviously see out of our windows.

"I know."

Sheila says, "When Amelia and I pass the Church of the Resurrection, I can hear music. It has a beautiful organ."

"Do you go to that church?"

"Every now and then. The organist is from Canada."

I remember Peter taking me by this Episcopal church a year or so ago. He peeked in. There was a Latin Mass going on with incense floating up to the ceiling. I wonder if they would acccpt me as a member. But then, am I a Roman Catholic? The boss is. Mrs. Rowley is a lapsed Catholic, and Caroline never goes, although the two women in my life do sometimes go on Christmas or Easter. But Mrs. Rowley prefers St. Ignatius Loyola, which the boss refers to as Saint Iggy's. She says she likes the interior architecture and doesn't like the Romanesque decoration of St. Jean Baptiste. The boss likes St. Jean.

On our way back from a weekend in Onteora, they give me a better seat. The car is filled with food, furniture, the boss's Callaway golf clubs, and clothes stuffed into leather carrier bags and black garbage bags. On the trip up to the northern Catskills, I was stuck curled up on the floor in one third of the rear of their rented Jeep, but on the way down, there's more room and I sleep on the rear seat itself, listening occasionally to Mr. and Mrs. Rowley talk about Caroline's boyfriend.

Since I'm not married, having been desexed many years ago, I'm not very interested!

I wander through the new room at 815. Out of the corner of my eye, I see a large dead brown bug holding onto the exterior screen outside. I'm always sorry to see fellow creatures die. How long will he or she stay there? The wind makes one of his legs move back and forth. It's spooky.

Then the boss and John Pieza, Mrs. Rowley's assistant, open the heavy window together, as it's too heavy for the boss to manage alone. The boss pokes at the bug with his gold-colored pencil through the screen, and all of a sudden my friend the bug flies away, and the boss sees him floating down fifteen floors to Seventy-Fifth Street.

I know the boss has been fishing for information. But then what can you expect from a writer looking for stories? He sounds so innocent, but I know better. He's trying to find out if Sheila's been married and, if so, how many times?

He says to Sheila, as she puts my collar around my neck, "Where do you live?"

"Second Avenue and Seventy-Second Street."

"When did you come to this country?"

"When I was twenty-one. I had a boyfriend in New Jersey, but I went to Vancouver first because I had a girlfriend there. My life has been a series of journeys. When I was a child, I wandered off three times and was lost. Life is a journey."

"The question is where is it a journey to?"

The boss thinks that's a pretty profound question and what a clever chap he is, but I know he's just paraphrasing Gertrude Stein's exchange with Alice B. Toklas: "What is the question?" "What is the answer?" But only basset hounds know what the answer is.

As I lie on my little couch in the living room, Peter walks by, gesturing with one hand toward me. "Crazy dog," he says.

I raise my left eyebrow.

Early this morning, as I entered the kitchen, planning to lie down on my pillow, I felt my right leg start to collapse under me. With some effort, I righted it.

Letitia says to the boss, "What a beautiful day. At last we have one."

I'm eating my mush.

"A beautiful day for the race."

"What race?"

"The human race."

The boss explains the joke to Letitia.

After Letitia understands what the boss says is a very old joke, she says, "I like the curve in Amelia's back between her hips and chest. At Oradell, there is a picture of a dog, and it says if you can't see this curve, your dog is in trouble."

"A hundred years ago," offers the boss, "young pretty girls were supposed to have hour-glass waists."

Peter comes in early in the morning and maneuvers around my bed. I am lying at an angle that would prevent me from getting up immediately and heading for the door, which I know is what he wants me to do. I lie there. Rowley first pulls up the blanket underneath me a little, but I can tell his heart is not in it. Then he has to go around to another side near my head and pulls another part of the blanket. I now have to get up and head down to the kitchen where I will await Sheila's eventual arrival.

Later in the morning Peter and Lady Terez are discussing something in which I am not interested and don't listen to when all of a sudden I let out a bark. I run toward Mrs. Rowley who falls to her knees and cuddles me. I wag my tail and squeal with delight. She kisses my head while lying on the carpeted floor beside her small desk. This goes on for quite a while, and I am very happy.

Mrs. Rowley does not come to bed until five o'clock. At seven, Mr. Rowley wakes up, and Mrs. Rowley starts screaming from the pain caused by sudden cramps. Mr. Rowley massages her thighs. I retreat to the kitchen. Mr. Rowley makes Mrs. Rowley a breakfast of two boiled eggs, American-style, freshly squeezed orange juice, one slice of buttered toast, and coffee with milk. He did not make any breakfast for me, although he did make the identical for himself. I guess I'd better get cramps next time.

I was getting tired of just lying there forever on the big dog bed beside Mrs. Rowley. I knew the boss was getting up every hour or so to go the bathroom. He was a light sleeper. So at 5:30 in the morning, I waddled around to his side of the bed until he saw in the dim light my white markings. He immediately got up, swinging his long legs out of the bed and tying up his pajama trousers string. He opened the door, and I went quickly down to the kitchen where I settled onto the other big bed. It would be a long wait until Sheila came for me shortly after nine o'clock.

That weekend, I was walking across the white sand behind Mrs. Rowley on Southampton beach. She suddenly turned around and wanted me to go back the way we'd come. But the wind was very strong, blowing right in my face, and the sand very soft and thick underfoot. I didn't want to move, but my mistress's powers of persuasion finally prevailed.

The boss has just returned from England and tells me that he saw Attila again at the end of the drive. Attila must be mourning his fellow pheasants that are being murdered in the surrounding countryside. One of the things I like about the boss is that he doesn't shoot, although he shamefully rents out his farmland to those who do.

Caesar had taken me to Oradell Hospital while the Rowleys were away, and I cried and growled most of the way there. Upon my return to 815 nine days later, I was wagging my tail happily.

Early in the morning, I ambled away from my bed as the boss stood over me. Mrs. Rowley who was still in bed, recovering from the flu, suddenly said, "I love you, Amelia."

I said nothing.

The boss said, "Say something, Amelia."

I did not.

Two men later appeared in my line of sight as I was resting on my round couch in the drawing room. I gazed at them, my ears hanging down appealingly. One was the boss. The other was a nice-looking young man. The latter came over and patted my head, saying "So this is Amelia." I appreciated the caress. The boss had forgotten to introduce me, but by overhearing snatches of their conversation, I learned the young man was Ellis Trevor. He is an agent for people like Mitt Romney, and he may sell my book to a publisher.

I wonder how much of the royalties I may have to end up sharing with Peter Rowley.

I overheard Letitia saying to the boss, "Amelia's brown spots of hair are not turning white. That's a good sign. Usually, when they're nearing death, the hair turns white."

I was being led to the kitchen door on a leash by Letitia when the boss said, "I wonder what Amelia is thinking."

Letitia said, "I wonder what dogs think when they sniff each other's behinds."

The boss replied, "I wonder, too."

It's none of their business!

I knew something was going on. When they locked me in the kitchen this morning and started assembling my stuff for Jay, I started to whine. Peter came in and caressed me. Then Jay arrived, and I started to bark. Peter came back in and stroked me. I stopped barking except for once or twice. Jay led me into the elevator, and I barked, but the boss waved to me from the kitchen door. I felt better, but I knew I was going away to Jay's house in Queens for the Christmas holidays. Will I ever see the beloved Rowleys again?

I whined when I first arrived at Jay's house, but he patted me, and I was glad I was there. I guessed he would tell the Rowleys over the telephone how happy I was with him before they left for the UK. The Rowleys were being delayed by reports of snow in England on top of the general incompetence of Heathrow Airport.

If Jay did tell Peter how happy I was, I figured he would become jealous, but I think he would also be happy for me.

I heard later that Caroline's boyfriend, Russell Boggess, was leaving the penthouse that morning when he spoke to a woman I guessed was Mrs. Haynes-Dale, who started complaining about my barks and wanted to know more about the construction in the studio. Russell politely told her nothing.

I am becoming very particular about the sort of cushion I sleep on in the kitchen when waiting to be taken out in the early morning by Carmen or Sheila. Rowley leaves the narrow thin one, but I prefer to lie on a loose small carpet on the kitchen floor. After a few days, Rowley gets the message and puts my big brown cushion on the floor. I climb onto it.

Rowley says to Sheila, "Where do you live again?"

I know Rowley already knows Sheila lives nearby.

"Seventy-Sixth Street and Second Avenue."

"Is it a rental or a co-op?"

"A rental."

"Have you been there a long time?"

"Yes."

Sheila holds open the kitchen door so Rowley can carry out a garbage bag. Sheila then takes me out, pulling me by my leash, but neither Rowley nor I are any the wiser about whether she's been married.

FURTHER ADVENTURES

Snow lay everywhere on the Morcott Hall grounds. Attila kept knocking with his beak against the French doors leading to the I'Anson's kitchen. Sandra opened a door. Attila fled. A little later, Sandra stepped out to the far end of the hedge to place some birdseed on the drive for Attila.

Mrs. Rowley does not trust Letitia. "She lies," I overheard her say. Peter doesn't trust her either.

There was the time that Peter was sure I had put on weight. So Pieza, who's paid a hundred dollars an hour as a computer consultant to the Rowleys, was asked to weigh me. He first weighed himself on the electronic scales. Then he picked me up in his arms and weighed me. Peter was not there, but later John told him, "Fifty-seven point nine pounds." Peter saw my previous weight was fifty-eight point six and was surprised.

He said to John, "That's some slight progress." Peter thought he was wrong about Letitia this time.

A few days ago, there was another scare to do with my health. Apparently, I was moving too slowly—me! I had never felt in finer fettle. To wit, as loyal servant to Mrs. Rowley, I have continued to bark whenever I see someone I have my doubts about.

Avra the vet came over, and I was given a couple of aspirins. I continued to maintain my daily regimen of sleeping twenty out of twenty-four hours a day. And then apparently I recovered, or maybe the human adults had just *imagined* all along that I was moving too slowly. I continue to walk, waddle, and occasionally run, usually when Mrs. Rowley calls me. And of course she cuddles me frequently. I like that.

And then I struck again! I refused to go back to the bedroom and sleep on my couch next to Mrs. Rowley and her husband. I stayed on my round bed in the drawing room. Terez came out during the night, but I wouldn't move. Then the boss came out at about one o'clock in the morning, but I still didn't want to move. And so he left me alone. Then the boss got up at six o'clock and caught me drinking my pee on that expensive oriental carpet in the living room. He kicked me gently in the behind, and I retreated to the kitchen where he usually puts me early in the morning.

Boss Rowley just came back from England. He avoided the royal wedding while he was there. He's a republican—not a member of the Republican Party but a believer in a republic as opposed to a monarchy. He played tennis the morning Kate and William spent millions of the taxpayers' pounds. As a basset hound, I must ask you, what has this couple ever done to deserve immense riches and fame?

Later the same day, Rowley drove to St. Neots and looked at his farms. There were long fields of green wheat waving in the wind. A hare jumped past, using its powerful hind legs to speed across the field. The boss described this marvelous scene to me, but I should like to have enjoyed it personally.

The human beings have discovered another basset hound. The boss and Mrs. Rowley just met Bosco. Who is Bosco? A male seventy-pound six-year-old dark brown and black animal who lives near Seventy-Sixth and Park. I've met him a few times. He tried to be friendly. I ignored him. From my lowly vantage point, his owner looks to be about forty, round-faced, curly blond hair, and friendly.

Walking with Sheila this morning, I saw a Labrador and snapped at him! After I came back to my apartment, I saw Mrs. Rowley in the hall in her filmy white nightgown and ran happily to her, wagging my tail. We love each other. "Darling, darling Amelia, I love you so much," she said.

Early the next morning, I woke up to a very dark bedroom. Mrs. Rowley and Mr. Rowley were asleep. The doors were open and except for one or two lights in the living room, there was only the early-morning ambient light. Without urinating, I wandered down to my other bed in the living room. An hour or so later, Mr. Rowley pulled up the blanket I was lying on, and I went into the kitchen. He barred my escape with the portable gate and closed the other kitchen door. End of story.

You can imagine my shock when I was still lying there at a quarter to nine in the morning, waiting for Sheila to come and take me out, when I heard a loud pop. Mrs. Rowley had been boiling eggs on the stove above me. She had gone off to a board meeting of our co-op. She wanted hard-boiled eggs. Then there was another loud pop. I could see bits of egg on the edge of the cooker. Then another one. Was I going to be burned up?

Finally Mrs. Rowley came flying through the kitchen door, screaming, "*Peter, why didn't you turn off my eggs? Idiot! Idiot!*" Then she realized her husband had not returned from his early morning tennis. She turned off the gas and gave me a hug. She started cleaning up. I could have been burned to death!

It nearly happened again two days later. The kettle was boiling away, but I could see the gas had not been turned up full blast. Caroline had put the kettle on this time. Then she had gone off to greet her potential future mother-in-law. This woman, a Mrs. Boggess from Chicago, the mother of Caroline's boyfriend, Russell, was coming for breakfast in the new studio upstairs.

Caroline had forgotten about the kettle. It kept sputtering away. I retreated to the other side of the kitchen. Finally, the boss opened the other door that leads into his office where he had been doing his exercises to avoid having a hip operation. He came in and turned off the kettle, saving my life.

I overheard Carmen, our part-time maid, saying to Peter about Mrs. Boggess, "She's a strong woman." Later, I was taken upstairs to meet the lady herself.

Panic! Alarm! And it didn't just affect Mrs. Rowley, Mr. Rowley, Caroline, and Letitia. It involved me, too. Though I took the news more calmly than the others, even though I was the one most affected. There's a bump on my back, and it's been growing. It's above the area where I had my disc removed by that doctor. As you will remember, I spent six pleasant weeks recuperating. Is it cancer? Letitia's eyes grew moist, and even a tear or two appeared, when Peter and Letitia were discussing the growth.

Letitia said, "You're not one of those families that kill off the pet when they hear the c-word?"

Peter said, "No, we're not going to euthanize her."

Letitia said, "I'm so relieved."

Avra the vet came and took a sample of my blood. Nobody asked my permission before she stuck a needle in me. But it didn't hurt much. Avra wanted me to go that afternoon to the east side hospital for an X-ray the following morning, telling Mrs. Rowley to not give me any food. But Mrs. Rowley forgot to tell Letitia, and the upshot was that my X-ray was postponed until the report on the blood test came in which I heard would be in five days.

So I went about my business, eating, sleeping, and going for walks. I even managed to urinate twice in the bedroom beside Mrs. Rowley in the early morning. Mr. Rowley had not taken me to the kitchen. Maybe he felt sorry for me and decided to let me revert to my not infrequent bathroom habits. Is Peter secretly happy that I may be approaching death? After all, he is a writer and he may try to take all the credit for our memoir if I'm not around. But most of the time, I think he wants me to live.

I saw that Mrs. Rowley was in tears. "I can't bear waiting five days to hear of the results of Amelia's blood test."

Mr. Rowley comforted her, putting his arms around her, and they hugged.

I feel fine, and I don't even notice the bump on my back.

I couldn't possibly have known that disaster was looming. Early this morning, Peter and Terez accompanied me in Caesar's big white SUV to the west side hospital where they had cut out the disc from my back two years before. Terez had insisted I sit on the back seat, my head on her lap, and Peter on the other side of me.

We waited until a nurse called Angela came, and then we waited some more. At one point, I headed out into the center of the lobby to greet a whitish bulldog. Peter held on to my leash as it started wrapping around Terez's neck.

"You're strangling me," she exclaimed. She ducked under the rope, and I exchanged nose rubs with the "bull."

Then Angela took us into a small examination room, and I snuggled under the chair where Terez was sitting. Peter dropped the leash. I headed out into the lobby. Terez rushed out to capture me. Then a Dr. Levy came. He was not the Dr. Seaman who had cut a hole in my back two years before. Levy was a pleasant, stocky man who confirmed what Terez and Peter already knew: he would take X-rays of my bump and chest, do a blood test, and cut a small slice out of my bump for a biopsy.

Terez and Peter insisted that Levy release me back into their care that evening, which Levy reluctantly agreed to. It was decided that Caesar would collect me, accompanied by Peter, if it were after seven as Terez was due at the annual meeting of our co-op. This was to be her last meeting before retiring.

Dr. Levy phoned the Rowleys at about 11:30 in the morning to say the X-rays had been done and the blood test completed, but the biopsy might have to be followed by radiation or surgery. After the phone conversation, Terez made it clear she was not going to allow them to cut a big slice out of me like the other hospital had done with Flora. Flora had died three months later.

In fact, they did cut a biggish slice out of me, which I did not exactly appreciate. At least it didn't compare with Flora, losing two-thirds of a paw, and I still have most of my back intact. Fortunately, it doesn't hurt due to the painkillers, but the Rowleys told Avra, my vet, referring to Dr. Levy, "It's a disgrace! He deceived us! The little biopsy is rather a big slice, and Amelia's bump is bigger than it was before the operation."

True, my bump is all swollen, and there's a huge swath of my beautiful fur gone, and for what? I know I only have some months to a year to live. Anyway, I'm back home, being snuggled by Mrs. Rowley and stroked by Mr. Rowley. And this morning, after a penitent Avra turned up, I had my first meal in twenty-four hours. Avra then personally took me out to the street, which she's never done before.

I'm feeling better today. It's not clear whether Dr. Levy and his team cut one big chunk out of my growth for a biopsy or did a number of small ones. Terez thinks I don't know how awful the red scar looks, but I am aware. In fact, I'm proud of it. It should scare away obnoxious people, and I still like to wag my tail to those I like.

When Letitia arrived this afternoon to take me out, it was raining slightly. She said, "I'm worried because Amelia's wound is not covered."

Peter said, "Take an umbrella."

"I have one. But I won't keep her out long—just until she does her business."

I returned to my apartment, more or less dry. The swelling of my bump is going down.

I overheard Dr. Levy and the Rowleys discussing my fate on the phone. Dr. Levy was proposing surgery, chemotherapy, radiation, and something else that I can't remember now.

None of these did I find very appealing, but Levy assured the Rowleys I would live six to twelve months longer. As for Mr. Rowley's suggestion (he insisted that Levy allow him to express his view) that I be allowed to die a natural death, the good doctor said I could be given painkillers if I were in pain. Both Mr. and Mrs. Rowley told him about Flora's last months and reminded him about the discomfort I suffered from the recent surgery that Levy had originally presented as a little biopsy.

Afterward, Terez and Peter reiterated that they preferred the natural option. Letitia arrived. I barked loudly a few times and then happily bounded out the back door before going to the street.

Today, the sun is shining brightly. Mrs. Rowley and Caroline had a fight over how many chairs and cushions along with a ladder could fit in Russell's car. Caroline was planning on driving Mrs. Rowley to Locust Valley where Caroline is buying a house with money given to her by Mr. Rowley. Why can't they buy me one too?

Weeping, Mrs. Rowley said she wanted to take me with her

or not go at all. After they left, I whined constantly despite the boss's attempts to soothe me. The boss was doing his exercises. Eventually, I stopped, and Sheila arrived to take me out. Carmen, our part-time maid, said, "Amelia's hair is growing back, and the swelling is going down." Sheila and Mr. Rowley agreed.

Half an hour later, Peter walked by me, saying "Crazy dog." I ignored him.

The Rowleys were about to leave for England, and I went off with Jay and his family to their home in Queens, my tail wagging happily. All three of the Rowleys were there to say goodbye to me as I went down the service elevator with Jay's family. I don't know their last name, but I like them.

After about a week, my back legs gave out. I guess it was my back and something to do with that nasty growth where they had operated three years before. I sensed that Mrs. Rowley in England was thinking about me.

I heard Jay call Letitia. Letitia was going to come and get me with Caesar and take me to that hospital on the west side. I heard some talk about steroids and helping me to urinate by squeezing. Anyway, I did No. 2 without any help.

Avra, my vet, is on jury duty, but she'll probably come and see me too. I miss the Rowleys.

I spent one night in the hospital—or was it two? Letitia came. Then she and Caesar took me back to Jay's in Queens. Caesar's a strong Peruvian and carried me. I don't feel too bad, but that growth won't go away.

Then yesterday morning, Jay and his family took me in their car back to my Park Avenue apartment. Mr. and Mrs. Rowley were there to greet me, but not Caroline.

Last night, I woke up at a quarter to five in the morning and pulled myself to the kitchen with my front legs, leaving a slight trail of blood. Lately, I have been dragging myself around a lot since my hind legs gave out. I'm depressed. Is this the end? This afternoon, Mrs. Rowley took me up to the penthouse where it's nice and sunny.

Today was Friday and the Rowleys went out to dinner with friends. I stayed in the penthouse, waiting for them to return. Then just before ten in the evening, a new doorman, Kevin, a summer intern from Ireland, carried me in his strong arms to the Rowleys' bedroom where I had a good night.

At eight the next morning, Mrs. Rowley got up and used a blanket to hold up my rear legs and behind and took me to the kitchen. I had a big accident of poo-poo and pee-pee, and Mrs. Rowley had to get more blankets and cushions for me. Then the service elevator broke down, so I won't be able to spend the morning on the sunny terrace by the penthouse until it's repaired.

I have stopped wagging my tail.

I can tell from the eyes of Peter, Terez, Caroline, and Letitia that they are thinking I may die soon. Perhaps they're planning on putting me to sleep—a euphemism that could apply to lots of different kinds of deaths: capital punishment, natural death in a hospital or rest home, casualty of war, or even victim of a car accident.

This morning, Terez carried my rear end in a blanket from the master bedroom to the door of Peter's office. She shouted at her husband. He rushed to open it. She brought more blankets to the kitchen for me, and I crawled to a spot near the kitchen door. I heard the boss approach as I was whining. He locked the kitchen door and stroked my ears. Then Terez appeared at the back door, returning from the basement. Peter unlocked the door but restrained Terez from entering until my head was safely out of the way. She left the kitchen, saying she'd put up the gate in front of the other door so I wouldn't crawl to the dining room. But she forgot, and I lay down on the dining room carpet.

This afternoon Avra, the vet, wearing a kind of safari outfit, appeared in my kitchen. That's a bad sign, I immediately thought. Caroline was there, too, as was Terez and Letitia. They began a discussion of whether and when I should live or die, and Letitia left by the kitchen door. I don't think my favorite dog walker likes these kinds of discussions, but if she had perhaps fed me a bit less food, I might be living longer. Peter appeared and leaned against the stone kitchen tabletop.

Avra said, "The cancerous growth on her back might explode."

Peter replied sharply, "You don't know that."

Caroline said, "Peter's writing a book about Amelia."

Terez said hysterically, "You'll have to put her to sleep."

Peter said, "We could let her live to Sunday."

Peter added, "How could you put her to sleep now? You don't have the equipment."

Avra replied, "It's out in my car. I have a car service waiting outside."

Peter nodded assent.

Terez did, too, and so did Caroline.

Avra and Terez carried me in my blanket to the center of the living room where I usually sit and placed me on the floor.

Then Avra stepped out while Terez lay on the floor, cuddling me. Caroline lay on the other side of me, holding my head.

Peter said to Caroline, "You never cared for her much."

Caroline retorted, "Why are you always putting me down?"

Peter denied this and went over to the other side of the carpet. He lay down on his side and started to stroke me.

Avra appeared holding a round patterned bag the size of a lady's evening bag with a zipper.

I stared into the eyes of Terez, Caroline, and Peter and glanced nervously several times at Avra who was kneeling next to my paralyzed rear legs.

I saw her push a needle into my right leg. Terez was holding me, Caroline was supporting my head and Peter was still gently stroking me. I began to feel sleepy. I felt a sudden shock of pain in my paralyzed leg.

Through the mist of the sedation, I heard Caroline say to Avra, "Have you ever done this before?" I heard Avra say, "Yes."

Then I felt another tiny prick in my ankle.

EPILOGUE: PETER'S STORY

All of us—that is to say, Terez, Caroline, and I—were at my house in England when Letitia phoned from New York to say Amelia's legs had given out at Jay's. It had taken Letitia several hours to figure out not to use the first "0" when making a transatlantic phone call to England. A few days later, in the Imperiale Hotel in Santa Margarita, Italy, where we had flown in a private jet via Genoa, Terez and I had one of the worst fights of our marriage over when we should return to New York to care for Amelia. After many harsh words, it was decided next morning to return to New York four days early.

While we were discussing Amelia's fate in the kitchen with Avra, I had considered asking that she be allowed to live until Sunday so that I could take some more photos of her in the sunlight on our penthouse terrace, but I did not feel the artistic merits of this book outweighed consideration of Amelia's quality of life and immediate future, however long that might be. So I remained silent.

While Avra, my wife, and daughter and I were waiting for Amelia to lay her head down on the brown and white pillow, Caroline or Terez remarked (I don't remember who), "Is this the way prisoners are executed?"

I said, "It's exactly the same."

Then Avra took a tiny clamp and placed it around Amelia's

leg after applying a tourniquet higher on the leg. She injected a needle attached to a thin plastic tube, which quickly filled up with Amelia's blood from a vein. She then attached another hypodermic with a reddish fluid to the other end of the tube and pushed down on the hypodermic. After about thirty seconds, Amelia suddenly twitched and the needle came out.

Terez said, "She's a fighter. She was the only one who survived when her mother and siblings died."

Avra tried to find another vein. After about a minute, she found a different spot and repeated the process. We waited. Amelia was clearly breathing. The phone rang, and I struggled to my feet, but the other person had hung up.

I had not been forewarned about what might happen if Avra came. I rang the River Club to say I would be late for my lesson. I had to change into tennis clothes. When I returned to the living room, I placed my hand on Amelia's side.

Terez said, "She's still breathing."

"No," I said, putting my palm on her lower stomach, "she's warm, but she's no longer breathing."

I left, and I heard that Jay, our doorman, carried her body down to Avra's car, tears in his eyes.

At a bit before ten in the evening, Terez returned to our bedroom, where I was already in pajamas under the duvet trying to go to sleep. She was crying. She had forgotten to tell Sheila we had returned from Europe a few days early, and Sheila had appeared in our living room, looking for Amelia.

The next morning, Terez said, "Amelia's and Flora's deaths reminded me of my mother's."

My psychotherapist called, and while telling him what had happened, I had to pause between sentences to conceal the sound of my voice breaking.

For some reason, I suddenly remembered how Amelia had slid down the Onteora staircase without a mark on her.

On Sunday, the very day I would like to have let Amelia live to, I took the A line elevator and encountered a pretty young woman holding on a leash a tiny, brown, furry dog.

"What kind of a dog is that?" I said.

"A toy poodle."

"We just put our basset to sleep two days ago." I gestured with my hands apart to show how long Amelia was.

"If you want to borrow my dog?" she said. I laughed.

On Monday—three days after Amelia left us—I still felt like crying when I thought of her. My friend, Nick Taylor, author of *A Necessary End*, emailed me, "So sorry to hear about your basset hound. Do the airlines waive ticket change fees in such cases?"

I emailed Nick back, "Although basset hounds are very important beings, unfortunately, the airlines don't equate them with us."

Steve, our big doorman, turned to me as I stepped out of 815 Park, "I'm sorry about Amelia." I replied, "Yeah."

Farther down Park Avenue as I walked south, I passed by Jane Sexton, who lives in 6C. She was walking her bulldog, Tallulah. Jane said with a sympathetic smile, "I'm sorry about Amelia." I answered with a gulp, "Yeah."

We went to Onteora for the weekend. I counted the steps Amelia had slid so smoothly down two years earlier—thirteen. I thought I saw her sitting on the grass behind the fence surrounding the swimming pool. We would often park her there so that she couldn't escape and possibly be hit by a car on the public highway about a quarter of a mile away. We returned late Sunday night from Onteora.

The next morning, I saw a black form on the carpet beside our bed, but I realized it wasn't her poo-poo. It turned out to be a gray glove my wife wears at night for her arthritis.

www.ingramcontent.com/pod-product-compliance
Ingram Content Group UK Ltd.
Pitfield, Milton Keynes, MK11 3LW, UK
UKHW041941190726
13854UKWH00004B/1723